To The 21st Century Christian Church:

HOW DID WE COME TO THIS?

The Christian Church: Identity in Flux!

BOB WALLACE: EMERITUS

WESTBOW
PRESS®
A DIVISION OF THOMAS NELSON
& ZONDERVAN

WestBow Press books may be ordered through booksellers or by contacting:

WestBow Press
A Division of Thomas Nelson & Zondervan
1663 Liberty Drive
Bloomington, IN 47403
www.westbowpress.com
844-714-3454

Scripture quotations are taken from the New American Standard Bible®, Copyright © 1960, 1962, 1963, 1968, 1971, 1972, 1973, 1975, 1977, 1995 by The Lockman Foundation. Used by permission.

ISBN: 978-1-6642-9701-2 (sc)
ISBN: 978-1-6642-9700-5 (e)

Library of Congress Control Number: 2023906502

Print information available on the last page.

WestBow Press rev. date: 04/12/2023

PREFACE

This book is dedicated 'unto the angels of the Christian Churches of the 21st century, and is borne out of deep concern for the work and mission that the Lord bestowed upon His angels, the Pastors, Messengers, and Overseers of His churches. It is a critical analysis of the seven basic flaws of the 21st church, and the responsibility of the under-shepherds whom God has placed as primary servants of the kingdom's business in His absence. It is not, and should not be taken as destructive criticism, but should be viewed constructively. Prayerfully, I have endeavored to bring into focus seven of the most devastatingly destructive problems confronting Christian churches in this coming decade. Those problems are: (1) the church as it relates to the use and abuse of drugs, and the devastating effect it has inflicted upon families and communities. (2) the church's failure to address the systematic genocide of young black men in America through the drug culture, gangs, and the legal system; (3) the churches that are suffering from a credibility crisis in the pulpit; (4) the total lack of discipline, morality, and respect in churches, and in public schools; (5) the warfare of denominational distinctions between purported Christian churches; (6) the improper utilization of church funds; (7) and finally, the lack of discipline in the churches, and parenting of our children in western society. There must be a realization that the same, or similar problems existed in the seven churches in Chapter 2 and 3 of the Book of Revelations, are prevalent to a greater extent in most present day churches. This series of messages are primarily dedicated to the teachers and pastors of the churches of the 21st century. There are many that are engaged in great works within their respective communities; but then there are some that are not. Just as Jesus was person oriented and not property oriented; likewise, this book expresses the love and compassion I feel for the Lord's people and the work that must be accomplished. I pray my love and compassion for the Lord Jesus manifests itself in the form of constructive criticism borne out of a love for the Lord's Pastors, messengers, and teachers of all Christian churches. The primary goal and purpose of this book is to open Christian hearts and minds to the true work the Lord Jesus has assigned for the angels of Christian churches of the 21st century. May the Lord Jesus richly bless all.

PROLOGUE

The words above are an indictment against the Church at Ephesus, and all Christian Churches that <u>left their first love</u>; and their first love must be for the One that loved us first. When one loves Christ first and above all others; then and only then, will one be empowered by the Holy Spirit to 'preach the gospel of Jesus Christ; His death, burial, resurrection, ascension, and return.' When empowered by the Spirit of Christ one accepts the great commission; to [1]"Go therefore and make disciples of all nations, baptizing them in the name of the Father, and of the Son, and of the Holy Spirit, teaching them to observe all that I have commanded you; and lo, I am with you always, to the close of the age." This failure to prioritize the love of Christ above all others is prevalent in many Christian churches today and it has resulted in "A Crisis in the Pulpit!!!"

---

[1] Mathew 28:19-20; P.815 (NASB)

A CRISIS IN THE PULPIT

Revelation 2:1-7; P.998 (NASB)
"To the angel of the church at Ephesus write: The
One who holds the seven stars in His right hand, the
One who walks among the seven golden lampstands,
says this: 'I know your deeds and your toil and
perseverance, and that you cannot tolerate evil men,
and you put to the test those who call themselves
apostles, and they are not, and you found them to be
false, and you have perseverance and have endured
for My name's sake, and have not grown weary. <u>But I
have this against you, that you have left your first love.
Therefore remember from where you have fallen, and
repent and do the deeds you did at first;</u> or else I am
coming to you and will remove your lampstand out
of its place-unless you repent. Yet this you do have,
that you hate the deeds of the Nicolaitans, which I
also hate. He who has an ear, let him hear what the
Spirit says to the churches. To him who overcomes,
I will grant to eat of the tree of life which is in the
paradise of God."

CHAPTER I

A Crisis in the Pulpit

It is evident by the recurring ecclesiastical horrors that are occurring, as focused upon by the visual media and the press, that there is a crisis33 in the pulpits of Christian churches in America. It is a crisis that must be confronted and removed for the Master's sake, and for the sake of all true believers. It is a crisis that impacts the very heart of Christ, who gave His life for His church. This crisis violates the honor and esteem of every obedient servant/angel of the Lord Jesus Christ. This crisis is "A CRISIS IN THE PULPIT." One of the most destructive occurrences in the Christian church is that of the servant/angel violating the sacred calling and trust that he received of the Lord Jesus. The real danger is that we have too many men in the pulpit that have called themselves; in order to serve themselves. If there is no conviction of an authentic calling, then that person is serving Satan, and none greater than himself. Once there is a conviction by the Spirit of a calling, it will result in a commitment that will be borne of obedience and love of the Lord Jesus Christ. If there is not a personal relationship with the Master, then you may have been called, but not by the Master. Unless you have the Spirit of Christ there can be no sincerity and/or truth in service. Perhaps you heard the voice of another master calling; hence, you are serving the wrong master. There seems to be an abundance of ecclesiastical aspirants in the world, and it seems as though the southern United States has the majority, and Texas receives a gold star. It has been said, 'shake any tree in Texas and a preacher will fall out of it.' It seems as if 1 out of 5 men you meet in Texas is a preacher, because many see the church as a means to hustle, a means to legally dupe people out of their income and property. The reason for the calling of preachers by the Lord is, not for personal gain; but to gain persons for Him to empower in His ecclesiastical war against evil by preaching the good news of the salvific works of the crucified Christ. The Bible says,[2] "How then will they call upon Him in whom they have not believed? How will they believe in Him whom they have never heard? And how are they to hear without a preacher?" Many of these quasi-ecclesiastical heralds of the faith have no relationship with Jesus, and preach what benefits their own agenda. They do not preach Christ and Him crucified, but preach the gospel of self and self-aggrandizement. It is the gospel of prosperity, and they are the ones who will become prosperous and affluent, but only for a season. They have become wealthy by performing, rather than preaching the gospel; and the crowds will usually follow an entertainer before they will follow a sincere God called preacher. The fault does not fall solely on these false prophets, but some of the onus is on us; who compose the body of Christ, because we refuse to test these men before we accept them. It is evident that if we do not try them, test them, validate their calling, check out their history, then the onus is on us. The Bible says, [3]"Do not lay hands on anyone too hastily (soon) and thereby share responsibility for the sins of others; keep yourselves free from sin." We accept too readily anyone that says "The Lord has called me to preach" only to find out later that the voice they heard was not the

---

[2] Romans 10:14; P.922 (NASB)
[3] I Timothy 5:22; P.967 (NASB)

Lord, but by that time we have 'a crisis in the pulpit.' There are three deadly sins that a Pastor/preacher/angel of the church can commit that will create 'a crisis in the pulpit'; and that is an inordinate desire for either one, or all of the following: <u>MONEY, SEX, and/or PRIDE!</u>

The golden lampstand was designed to emit light, and reveal that which was previously in the dark. The 'angels' of the local Christian churches must become lampstands for the body of Christ that shed light upon the darkness of those who claim a spiritual calling to serve our Lord Jesus Christ. This must be accomplished by testing, trying and observing the one professing a call to special service. ' A crisis in the pulpit' can be avoided if we place obstacles of faith that will test their sincerity, commitment, and resolve; especially, as it pertains to what their lips have proclaimed. [4]If they have a history of being debt ridden, a sparse track record of employment, and constantly borrowing and not repaying; then why would you allow this person to serve on the church's finance group? Why place them in a position where they are continually tempted by their weakness. You don't put a starving man in a warehouse filled with food, and then tell him not to eat anything. A prime example of this teaching is that of Judas Iscariot, who betrayed the Master. You might say, "wasn't Judas chosen by the Lord and allowed to serve as the treasurer?" Judas was chosen, even though the Lord knew he would betray Him; but those who would come after Judas could not say that the Lord is not a God of many chances. Judas had the opportunity to repent and change, but chose the path of unrighteousness and condemnation. [5]John, in retrospective meditation, recalls the past conduct and nature of Judas was that of a 'thief'; and that is what he was and that was what he did. Judas was given greater privilege and responsibility than most of the disciples, but the [6]"love of money" ultimately led to his demise. When Mary of Bethany poured precious, expensive ointment upon our Master, and anointed Him with its sweet fragrance; Judas objected

---

[4] Reference: I Timothy 3:1-10; P.966 (NASB)
[5] Reference: John 12:6; P.876 (NASB)
[6] Reference: I Timothy 6:10; P.967 (NASB)

with the pretense that the precious ointment could have been sold and the money could be used to help the poor. But almost as a footnote John says, [7]"because he was a thief, and he had the bag." Judas, though faustian, was called to follow Jesus, but he sought the riches of the world, rather than the treasures of the kingdom of heaven. One of the great failures of the church today is that too many Pastors/angels have their hands in the 'bag'. They have, and control access to the funds of the church, and the temptation to misuse these funds is sometimes too great to resist. The misuse and misappropriation of church funds becomes 'a crisis in the pulpit.' It is a crisis that comes from a failure of church administrators to 'try them and test them'; to know as much as possible about who you are trusting with the Lord's funds, be it Pastor or laymen.

INTERLUDE # 1

We must recognize that not everyone that answers a calling, has received the calling of the Lord Jesus; however, it has been a failure on the part of the saints in authority in the church to ensure that the calling is authentic. It appears that anyone that comes before the church and testifies that they have been called to preach, we do not hesitate to start referring to them as 'Reverend'. We apply the term so readily, and so irreverently that it has minimal self efficacy, or personal import. By the way, the Bible says, [8]"holy and reverend is his name"; but truly there is none worthy of being reverent but God. The Apostle Paul tells Timothy, his son on ministry, [9]to 'Lay your hands on no man suddenly'; but rather, 'try them, put them to the test' to see if they are authentic and sincere to a calling. If they are truly God called, time and the Holy Spirit will reveal the truth. Know this, that the title of "Reverend" is an earned title paid for by a life lived in holiness and

---

[7] Reference: John 12:6; P.876 (NASB)
[8] Reference: Psalm 111:9; P.498 (NASB)
[9] Reference: I Timothy 5:22; P.967 (NASB)

obedience to the One who called, and to whom you answered. The one who called is not your earthly Pastor/preacher, not the deacon group (Board), not even the congregation (membership), but He is Jesus the Christ, the One who gave Himself for you, and He is the One who's call you have answered. If you are true to Him, you may never be wealthy, or famous, or even a Pastor; but you will be rewarded above all that you ever desired. That is true because there is a direct correlation between blessing and obedience. If you are called and are obedient to that call, then you will accomplish whatever the charge of your calling might be, whether great or small, but your reward will be great.

Meanwhile, back to the subject of 'a crisis in the pulpit;' and how it relates to the misappropriation of funds. How should the funds of the church be administered, and by whom? The Bible principal speaks of [10] 'men who have an honest report, a good reputation'; in other words, check them out before you ordain them to that lofty position, be sure that they have met the test of honesty and sincerity. There should never be one party access to church finances, and it is better that the Pastor/angel has no access, if possible. Collections, accounting, counting, depositing of funds should be accomplished in the presence of two or more persons. This would eliminate any possibility of collusion or conflict, but if it is necessary that the Pastor has access, he should always insure that at least two other signatures, or eye witnesses be required in all financial transactions of the church. No one person should bear the burden of being accountable for the funds of the church. This business principle is established in the Bible when Paul speaks of the collection of funds by the church at Macedonia for the relief of the Church at Corinth, [11]"first they gave themselves to the Lord,.......we have sent along with him (Titus) the brother whose fame in the things of the gospel......taking precautions so that no one would discredit us in our administration of this generous gift; for we have regard for what is honorable; not only in

---

[10] Reference: I Timothy 3:1-10; P.966 (NASB)
[11] Reference: II Corinthians 8:5-:24; P.941-942 (NASB)

the sight of the Lord, but also in the sight of men. We have sent with them our brother, whom we have often tested... .... As for Titus, he is my partner and fellow worker among you; as for our brethren, they are messengers of the churches, a glory to Christ." Paul sought to eliminate any derision and/or conflicting problems concerning the funds being collected for the saints at Corinth. He was sending Titus along with two faithful brothers that had been tested in the fires of evangelism with Paul and Titus. No one person should ever have access to Church funds, not because of distrust, but because it is the right way according to the Word of God. Oh, and by the way, do not issue an unlimited credit card to anyone in the church that is backed by the general fund of the church.

If the Pastor is on salary, stipend, or cash, let him obtain His own credit cards; create a separate account for petty cash, gasoline allowance, and miscellaneous expenses. Major long term indebtedness or contractual expenses pertaining to credit create a separate body of trustees to personally handle issues of long term indebtedness. Now unless I am amiss, the Pastor/angel of the church must have access to all financial records in order to lead, guide, plan, and budget for his own authority, and to inform the church periodically concerning the business of the churches finances. The moral lesson about the church's money is this: if you place anyone, who has no money, in charge of the money, then he or she who has no money, will have the money, and the money will be no more.

INTERLUDE #2:

The local church must also realize that calling someone from a 'far country' does not negate that they also have a history, and should be thoroughly investigated before accepting them as a potential Pastor. Many times you have within your church a God called preacher that you have known, and you already know, you know his family, raised in the neighborhood, that has been faithful and true to their calling; but because you know their father and their mother, and their brothers, and their sisters, the administrators fail to even seriously consider them. The asininity of that approach is that you already know this person, the good, the bad, and the ugly; but you call someone from afar based on a resume', or recommendation from an outside source. Jesus was confronted with that same type of hometown bigotry; since his neighbors in His hometown knew his family, they believed that knew all there was to know about Him. The Bible says,[12] "Jesus went out from there and came into His hometown; and His disciples followed Him. When the Sabbath came, He began to teach in the synagogue, and the many listeners were astonished, saying, "Where did this man get these things, and what is this wisdom given to Him, and such miracles as these performed by His hands? Is not this the carpenter, the son of Mary, and brother of James and Joses and Judas and Simon? Are not His sisters here with us?" And they took offense at Him. Jesus said to them, "A prophet is not without honor except in his hometown and among his relatives and in his own household." This kind of bigotry is like a two edged sword, it cuts going and coming. Could it be that they knew that Jesus also knew them and their not so pristine lives. They thought they knew Him, even after He exposed a Jesus that was awesomely gifted, a Jesus that they had not seen before; and though He exhibited Wisdom and miraculous deeds, they could not overcome their hometown familiarity with His family. So a preacher/servant is oft times not considered because the authorities of the church look past their dedication and service to the church, and perhaps familiarity breeds contempt; so they don't even consider the there is one among them that is worthy, and so they call an unfamiliar one from the far country.

There is another 'crisis in the pulpit' that is having scandalous and shameful repercussions upon the church; and a negative effect as it pertains to the evangelical mission of the church. It is the crisis of **"Sex and the Pulpit".** Sex is the primary tool that Satan uses to try

---

[12] Mark 6:1-6, P.821 (NASB)

and destroy the soul saving works of the church. No other horrendous deed cripples and hinders the propagation of the body of Christ than that of the Pastor/preacher who is engaged in an illicit sexual affair with a member or non member. If they are married or not; whether it is adultery, fornication, sodomy, or homosexuality, it destroys the credibility and authority of the church's mission and witness to the unbeliever as it pertains to the saving grace of our Lord and Savior, Jesus the Christ. We love to debate which of the aforementioned sins is greater than the other; but they are all equally detrimental and destructive to the kingdom. It is a deceptive argument that Satan uses to create schism and cliques among members in the church. ALL SIN IS UNDER THE SAME PENALTY, DEATH! [13]"For the wages of sin is death; but the free gift of God is eternal life in Christ Jesus our Lord." There are no degrees of sin or death, sin and death are absolutes. Almost sin is not sin, almost death is not death; and there is no purgatory, death is the reward for all sin; BUT, thank God for the buts in His word, **but** the gift, the grace of God given to all who would believe in the Son is eternal life. Stop trying to align God's word with the world's amoral perspective; we, as Christians are called to persuade the world to align itself with the morality of Christ Jesus. Clearly sex is one of Satan's most effective means of destroying the credibility of the evangelical effort of the Pastor/preacher. He knows that one of the strongest and most difficult natures that God has given to mankind, especially men, is the need for sexual gratification. The Pastor/preacher is constantly appearing before the church as a model and example of what a man ought to be, whether he is, or isn't is relevant. So many times women fall in love with the Pastor, rather than the Savior. Many of them set out intentionally to entice him, and many times, if he refuses or rejects them; she, like Jezebel, will seek to destroy him. Even the strongest of men, caught in a moment of temptation, or spiritual weakness can make a misstep; sin and succumb to vain desires in the passion of the

---

[13] Romans 6:23, P.919 (NASB)

moment. Satan has a tendency to place the opportunity of that which would be most difficult to resist at your disposal; the very one that you know you desire in your heart and mind, and now you are alone in a secluded, secret place, why not? And because their commitment to their calling is not anchored to 'the solid rock', they succumb to the wiles of the devil. Some of the world's greatest ministries, and churches have been destroyed by what seemed to be, God's gifted men and ministries; and were torn asunder by a disciple of 'Jezebel'. Perhaps even Adam's downfall was his love of Eve; we know of Samson and his fascination and lust for Delilah; David had a fixation on the body of Bathsheba that he could not overcome; Ahab was weak for the love of Jezebel; Mark Antony and Cleopatra; yes, women of beauty who beguiled men away from their destiny to sin and death. Women that have been desired by the gods, even the[14]"sons of God saw that the daughters of men were beautiful; and they took wives for themselves, whomever they chose." Many men have lied about their calling because they saw preaching as a means, not only to acquire money, but to acquire sex. There is a four to one ratio of women to men in the church, and some men see the admiration that some of the sisters have bestowed on the Pastor/preacher, so some of these brothers seek to take advantage of the situation. Many of the brothers in the church are there to take advantage of a surplus of women in the prime of their lives; and do just as much damage to the church as a wayward Pastor. Many of them are married, and hold a position of authority in service at their church; such as Deacons and Trustees. We need to be reminded occasionally [15]that whatever is done in the dark, will soon be revealed by light. Sex and the pulpit will continue to be problematic and destructive to the Pastors and churches, it will continue to create a crisis in the pulpit.

---

[14] Genesis 6:2; P.4 (NASB)
[15] Reference: Luke 8:17; P.843 (NASB)

INTERLUDE #3:

The modern day neo-christian church speaks very sparingly about sin; it tells the world what the Lord has done for us by grace and faith in Christ Jesus, but the acknowledgment of one's sins and repentance is not part of the new age Pastor/preacher's art of persuasion. This new age generation ignores sin and hell, as if they do not exist, and our mega-churches are filled to capacity with individuals that have never acknowledged their sins; and have no fear of going to hell. Sin has always had consequences, and to ignore them does not negate the inevitable consequences in this life, and the next. The Pastor/preacher that fails to preach and teach the detrimental effects of sin; and the consequence of unrepented sin apart from Christ Jesus the Lord is not true to His calling. So we have people joining the local churches that have never received the Lord Jesus as their Savior, nor have they repented of their sinfulness. We preach Christ Jesus crucified, died, buried, and risen; and never relay the message that He died to take our sin of death upon Himself; so that all who believe in Him might receive eternal life. [16]"The wages of sin is death, but the gift of God is eternal life." The gift that secures eternal life is God's only begotten Son, Jesus the Christ. [17]"For God so loved the world that He gave His only begotten Son, that whoever believes in Him shall not perish, but have eternal life." Jesus Christ is the propitiation, which secures mercy for sinners (all) by grace, which is without cost; because He first loved us. He does for us what we could not do for ourselves, and we should be thankful. Sin and hell are real as a condition, and a place, respectively. Yes hell is real and it is the abode and destination of all that remain under the penalty of unrepented sin, and have not received the efficacious sacrificial gift of the Son of God, Jesus Christ. If there is no hell, there can be no heaven; and since I choose to believe there is a heaven, then there must be a hell. [18]The Bible speaks of

---

[16] Romans 6:23; P.919 (NASB)
[17] John 3:16; P.866 (NASB)
[18] Reference: Luke 16:22-25 (NASB)

hell, sometimes rendered by the word Hades, which is the realm of the souls that have died, and in that place there is a place of torment and a place of comfort, separated by a great gulf which no soul can cross. If the consequences of unrepented sin renders one to the abode of torment in hell; and the repentance of sin and acceptance of the salvific work of Christ is to be present in a place of comfort in Christ; WHAT IN HELL DO YOU DESIRE?

Finally there is 'a crisis in the pulpit' created by Pastors/ preachers that are lofty, heady, and imbued with inordinate pride and self-aggrandizement. They have rendered themselves spiritually ineffective, because they have been blinded by the light of their own self appointed significance. They know that they do not serve God, but act as though the Lord is their servant; rather than them serving the Lord! Oh, you do know that there are some good shepherds; and oh yes, there are some bad shepherds, and not all shepherds serve the same Master. There are those who have become religious entertainers that prey on the spiritual ignorance of the masses. They camouflage their inadequate preparation and training, do not preach the uncompromising Gospel of the Lord Jesus Christ; but they expose clever cliches with highly emotional bravados, known as [19]'whooping.' Sometimes the people become so accustomed to this style of preaching that they believe there has been no preaching until there is 'whooping'; however, we should not be too concerned with how the message is delivered, but be concerned about the message. It has been said that a good whooper can preach any message other than Christ, and people will shout all over the church. I contend that if there is no preaching of the salvific works of the Lord Jesus the Christ, then your shouting is in vain. If Christ is preached; Him crucified, dead, buried, and risen and how that relates to my sinful condition, my situation, and this is the message prior to the whooping, then there is a reason to be joyous.

---

[19] Definition: Whooping Is a term derived from a popular method of preaching, primarily in predominantly black churches, in which the orator applies a rhythmical tune in their vocalization that usually begins in a low rhythmic monotone and escalates to a crescendo of emotional excitement.

You see, whooping is the celebration of deliverance by[20]'Him who has called you out of darkness into His marvelous light.' Whooping is a closing exaltation and celebration of the mercy and grace that the Lord Jesus has bestowed on us. Whooping is an option of a particular style of preaching, but before the whooping, you need to inform the church why you are celebrating. Many of us have been conditioned into believing that if the preacher does not whoop or sing us a sermon, then He has not preached. Many of those in the pews neither hear, nor respond to the message until the first quivering trill in the preacher's voice. The whooping preacher takes us on a journey that begins with that rhythmical, emotional, gradual crescendo that rises ever so slowly to the apex of our spiritual expectations; and before we know it, we are caught up in the excitement of the moment with amens, and hallelujahs! The remarkable thing is that most never heard or understood a word that was spoken; but man, it 'sho' did sound good'. So the church has traditionally accepted the whooper of the Word, in opposition to the teacher of the Word. Understand this, [21]"preaching is the power of God for salvation to everyone that believes", and teaching brings understanding, trust, and spiritual maturity. Jesus sat and taught His disciples to bring spiritual maturity and understanding to them concerning His mission during His incarnation. There is too much entertainment coming from the pulpit, and it is creating 'a crisis of credibility of the pulpit'. Some members of the churches have been in the local church for decades and are still being nourished with milk rather than the solid manna of the Word of God. Many are still babies because the Pastor can carry and lead babies anywhere he so chooses; but if you are maturing in the Word you must stop crawling and begin to walk, and if you walk, you can go where the Truth leads. [22]Once you know and obey the Truth, then you are free, because the Truth will set you free. There are plenty of entertainers and entertaining in the church:

---

[20] Reference: I Peter 2:9, P.987 (NASB)
[21] Reference: Romans 1:!6, P.915 (NASB)
[22] ; Reference: John 8:32, P.872 (NASB)

[23]Oh!, the world is hungry for the living Bread, lift
the Savior up to see; Trust Him and do not doubt
the words that He said, "I'll draw all men unto me.

Lift Him up! Lift Him up! Lift Him up! When you lift Jesus up
to the world you will experience the difference between feeling good,
and joy unspeakable, joy that will sustain you no matter the issue or
situation, joy that is eternal, joy that comes from a relationship with
the Master, joy because of the mercy and grace that the Lord has
bestowed, joy because you bask continually in the Light of His love,
joy for the foretaste of His presence now, joy for the fullness that is
to come, joy that allows me to bear the burdens of this life in silent
expectation, joy that allows me to broadcast the blessings of the Lord
with jubilation, joy is what comes to my heart when I think about the
goodness of Christ, and sing praises to His name; so the conclusion to
all this joy that I have, I don't really need a preacher to have joy, I can
have Joy with the Father, the Son, and the Holy Spirit all by myself.
Oh, praise His name forever and ever!

---

[23] Reference:The New Baptist Hymnal; "Lift Him Up", by Johnson Oatman, Jr.;
Copyright 1977, #411

CHAPTER II

The Great Emasculation Proclamation!

Revelation 2:8-11;P.999 (NASB)
"And to the angel of the church at Smyrna write:
The first and the last, who was dead, and has come
to life, says this: I know your tribulation and your
poverty (but you are rich), and the blasphemy by
those who say they they are Jews and are not, but
are a synagogue of Satan. Do not fear what you are
about to suffer.

Behold the devil is about to cast some of you
into prison, so that you will be tested, and you will
have tribulation for ten days. Be faithful until death,
and I will give you the crown of life. He who has an
ear, let him hear what the Spirit says to the churches.
He who overcomes will not be hurt by the second
death."

Philippians 3:13-14;P.955 (NASB)
"Brethren, I do not regard myself as having laid
hold of it yet; but one thing I do, forgetting what lies
behind, and reaching forward to what lies ahead, I
press toward the goal for the prize of the upward call
of God in Christ Jesus."

PROLOGUE:

The Church of Smyrna was being persecuted from within and
without. The Judaizers were teaching a doctrine that was contrary
to the teachings of the Apostle Paul; 'which was that salvation was
by faith and grace born of belief in the efficacy of the redemptive
salvific sacrifice of Jesus the Christ. These legalists followed Paul
relentlessly teaching the gospel of works. Many followers of Christ
were being killed and cast into prison because of their faith; and the
battle continues today when many of the black and brown brothers
are killed, and cast into prison based on discrimination, poverty, and
ignorance! It is a modern day systematic emasculation of minority
men that is designed to render them impotent, null and void. This
systemic affront to black and brown males is subtly being enforced, and
engrafted into the social and religious construct of America and the
world. It is the manifesto of "The Great Emasculation Proclamation!"

The Great Emasculation
Proclamation!

One of the most horrendous, hideous acts that is occurring in
the world today, and especially in America; (the home of the brave
and the free), is the systematic emasculation of black men relative
to their families, and their lack of authority in their communities.
Consider all the "generations of men" within the context of the

totality of man's existence; black men are truly [24]"The Endangered Species", and has been even before the institution of slavery in the Americas. When President Abraham Lincoln signed the manifesto of the 'Emancipation Proclamation'; "we hold these truths to be self-evident that all men are created equal", the majority of the states in America, both the North and the South, devised systems to perpetuate the emasculation of the black male. The predominantly white anglo-saxon male political and business systems set up barriers to prevent the acceptance of black men as free and equal entities. It was somewhat subtle in the Northern states, and extremely severe in the Southern states of America. I propose that after the legal abolition of slavery in America, emancipation was not the order of the day; but a purposeful emasculation black men from all that a purported free society could offer the newly freed slaves. They were systematically castrated, 'deballed' metaphorically speaking, and in some cases in actuality, removed from the privileges offered to free men. The newly emancipated slave was castrated of all that makes a man, a man; he was treated positionally subordinate to black women, because he could not own land, had no valid means for income, had no position of authority; and he was stereotyped as lazy, shiftless, irresponsible, undependable, and sexually animalistic by nature. The black female; however, was rendered somewhat of a lesser evil than the black male, but she was less likely to be violent; she was often violated sexually, accepted as nannies, cooks, and general household help at a less than modest fee. So, as a result of the perpetuation of this overt doctrine of subterfuge, these acts of discrimination were adopted by the majority of white America after the Civil War. It was a vain attempt to try and justify the emasculation of an entire race. The Confederate States of America's slave owners, after the enactment of the Emancipation Proclamation, could not sustain their lifestyles with a labor force that had to be paid. So, they devised a judicial system that would require that local prisoners, composed primarily of the newly freed slaves, would be

---

[24] Reference: "The Endangered Species", Documentary-by Bob R. Sander, (KERA-TV, Channel 13 PBS), 1987

required to work in the fields of plantation owners. So nothing really changed in the south until the mechanization of agriculture in the 20th century was introduced. The judicial and law enforcement systems became the driving force behind emasculation of black and brown males in America, and a great deal of the injustices heaped on men of color today is tainted by the aforementioned prejudicial practices.

The emasculation of black men disavows fatherhood, and promotes a matriarchal family system that is purposely designed to prevent black men from having any authority as head of their household. Yes, the political system and the power structure, which is predominantly under the control of white anglo-saxon protestant males, is a great hindrance to the emancipation of black men; but if you are a child of God, you have been called to a higher calling, a calling that will allow us to resume our designated purpose and position in our families and communities; and we must refuse to wallow in self pity and despair; if you are a black man that hasn't been emasculated, castrated, denigrated to the point of no return; then stand up and become all that you can be in the Lord Jesus Christ. The great emasculation proclamation can be defeated by the power and will of the almighty Jesus the Christ.

The great emasculation proclamation conspiracy is an assault against black men as head of household by preventing them access to the economic mainstream of the white anglo-saxon dominated economy. This was a conscious and visible affront to systematically render the black man impotent, useless, and dependent in America. The white male dominated businessmen and landowners sought to maintain the status quo of a cheap labor force, and to maintain dictatorial power and control over the newly freed black populus after the "Emancipation Proclamation" had been ratified. The myriad of laws and ordinances passed primarily by the 'confederate states' of the south were designed specifically to render the 'Emancipation Proclamation' of those of African heritage in America null and void, of no effect. The modern day assault on voting rights is borne of the same ideology. During the post Civil War era of extreme fear and racism;

the predominantly white anglo-saxon male politick enacted rules that established the new 'separate but unequal' system of apartheid. The white populous of the north merely stated on paper that blacks were free, but 'not as free, as we.' To render the black man economically impotent was the manner in which white America would render them utterly impotent in their own community. America would become the 'home of the brave and the racist free'; but only the white populace would fall under the banner of the highest freedom and equality. The illogic was, "If he has no job, then he has no money, no property, no pride, no self efficacy," no authority; thus, he will be relegated to the abyss of despair and utter worthlessness to himself and his family. The effects of this systematic racism has been perpetuated to this day; it is present in the schools, business, politics, government, and especially law enforcement. This is America, the land of opportunity; clothed in the lavishness of materialism; draped in the cosmetics of abundance; embellished as 'a land flowing with milk and honey'; blessed by God above all nations; and yet, white America embraces the subtle philosophy of the "Emasculation Proclamation" of its black quasi-citizens.

America is suffering from a callous heart, because its arteries have become clogged by an irrational fear of that which it has suppressed since the institution of slavery was first imposed. Surprisingly a great number of white Americans believe that racism no longer exists; and I agree that for them that is true, it no longer exists; yeah, and has never existed for them. If you have never had to confront a racist situation, moment, or person; then racism does not exist for you. Racism is only relevant to the perpetrator and the victim; the perpetrator who commits the act of racism, and the victim who is the brunt of the act of the racist. Some perpetrators are often unaware that they are racist, many believe they have always treated blacks fairly; and for many that is true. It is true because many have not completely thought the process through. They seem to have, when they truly examine their inner philosophy concerning race, a <u>"but clause"</u>; and it is usually supported by racist illogic. I worked with white men, as an only minority for many years; one of those, in particular, was one of the nicest, kindest, generous, Christian men with whom I have ever been associated. He, when discussing the race issues during that day and time, would say, "I don't have anything against brown or black people, we are all equal in the site of the Lord; integration in schools, housing, work, business, religion, etc.; and then he would introduce his "but clause"; but I don't want my daughter marrying a black, Mexican, or Asian man. I did not challenge him on that point because I recognized that he really would have no real control over who his daughter married; and no matter the genetic composition of his grandchildren, as a Christian, he would still love them. Unless I am amiss, I too have heart trouble, I have a "but clause"; I have the same basic testimony of my friend; however my "but clause" is not interracial marriage. I can interact with most people, "but" I don't trust white men until I get to know them, and then I still have my doubts. America's heart trouble is systemic and the heart will die if the arteries are not cleared of the plaque of racism. The removal of the plaque of racism in America is perpetual and it is painful; and it is not a one way street. We black men must also remove the plaque of racism from our own hearts. We must learn to forgive, and put behind us that which occurred in the past, and look forward toward the future, and run toward the goal that God has placed before us'. We must strive to gain a higher calling that is in Christ Jesus, the Lord.

What Christian black and brown men must realize is that they have been called to a higher calling, and buried deep within their subconscious is a [25]"a gentle blowing", that speaks to their hearts that a change is still coming. Yes, black lives matter; but, in reality, all lives matter. However, there is a disproportionate number of young unarmed black men being killed by white law enforcement personnel under disputable circumstances.

---

[25] I KIng 19:12; P.294 (NASB)

INTERLUDE #1

Behold! Black christian men must come face to face with their own shortcomings in dealing with the adverse circumstances that present themselves in this current aura of subtle racism. We have been called to a higher destiny, than to that of this world. Our state and condition in society is, in part, to be laid at our feet. No one can rob us of our dignity, no one can emasculate our masculinity, but we can voluntarily give it away. I submit to you that circumstances purposely perpetrated upon us in America, that sought to emasculate us by force, was accomplished by a cardinal lack of resistance by us. We relegated the 'man' to the shed, and took on the mantle of the 'boy'; though many died in their attempt to refute the systematic stereotyping that labeled all black men as inferior and worthless. There is a 'higher calling' that now, in this day and time, we need to stand and be counted as men, not boys. We, especially Christian men, must be accounted as men. We must hold our heads high, and look our white brothers in their eyes, and say, "I am a man and I demand respect as a man; and I refuse to be emasculated by this society or any other." We must demand, not only that black lives matter, but proclaim from the mountain tops that my life matters, and all life matters. It matters because I was bought at great cost to my Lord and Savior Jesus Christ. Bought and paid in full, so that I might stretch toward the mark of a higher calling of God in Christ Jesus.

There is no greater farce in America than the current judicial system that is the primary tool that racist have employed to emasculate, render impotent, the black and brown men. Only one law enforcement officer, in all of the videotaped incidents that revealed an unarmed black male being shot to death, yes, one, to this date, has been indicted, tried, and found guilty in any court of America. Even when the video shows the vivid evidence of what happened, the Grand Juries, and District Attorneys, delay and attempt to find loopholes in the law to justify murder. They are incognitant of the pain and trauma perpetrated on the loved ones of these victims whose cardinal guilt is being a black male. It is as though the loved ones of the victim are found guilty of being a relative of the deceased; and then sentenced to the prison of heartache and despair while the murderer is set free with a 2 to 4 week paid leave (vacation). This is justice in America, the home of the brave and not so free. The 'emasculation proclamation' is white America's manifesto of a subtle, genocidal declaration of eradication of the black male's authority and effectiveness in society.

INTERLUDE #2

There is an underlying morbid fear of black men by the white males in America; a fear that in an equal arena of competition for authority and status, they (white males) would be the primary loser. It is a fear that is not founded on facts, but on preconceived superstitions, and ethnic racial stereotyping. It is an attempt to simplify and categorize a whole race with simplistic labels in order to maintain a state of homeostasis of self. White America has become so entrenched in that comfort zone; and they stand firm and say, "I shall not be moved." It is as though their cognition has been encased in cement, eyes blinded by fear, ears sealed with hate; and hearts stymied by the fear of the unknown. Oh, if all men truly would know this Jesus who is the epitome of love incarnate; He would emasculate the corruptness of their hearts, and set them free from all of their burdens of sin and racism.

The black men who have been victims of the great 'Emasculation Proclamation', know that all of the burden of guilt is not on our white brothers alone. We have our own faults and shortcomings because we have by our own volition fallen into the traps that have been set before us. So we choose to be complicit to joining the do nothing crowd, as opposed to the group of believers and achievers in society. We choose football, basketball, track and field, baseball, tennis, and promiscuous sexual activity as our priority and high calling in life. The system encourages us to pursue those routes to success, but it doesn't reveal the odds of you being successful in these. If you haven't noticed that those in charge of your education do not interfere with the foolishness of those who are loud and obnoxious in school; they have resolved that because you are a black male, that 35% or more of you are either going to prison, or already in prison from ages 18 to 30; another 15% will be inadequately educated; another 8% are unemployable for a multitude of reasons; another 10 to 12% are slaves to gangs and/or the illegal drug economy of the nation. That is approximately 70% of the black male population that has been rendered useless by the American standard to attain legitimate, viable success. It is incumbent upon us as black men to improve our own merits by choosing to pursue the weightier matters in preparation to succeed in life. The very base of that improvement has to come from men who discipline their children in the home. We need black men to accept the banner of responsibility and authority in the home. The onus of our responsibility is manifested in our 'response' to God's 'ability'.

[26]"Now to Him who is able to do far more abundantly beyond all that we ask or think, according to the power that works in us." Yes, it is a fact that the system is biased against black and minority males, but we must put forth the necessary effort to overcome those obstacles that are placed before us. The governance of men has never, and never will be unbiased in its treatment of its people. If we understand that concept, we, as Christian men, must recognize that we are called to a higher calling of a positive response to situations and circumstances that we can't control. We have been called to a higher calling than prisons, gangs, drugs; and deserting our responsibilities to be fathers to our children. [27]"Let us not lose heart in doing good, for in due season we shall reap if we do not grow weary; so then, while we have opportunity, let us do good to all people, especially to those who are of the household of faith."

Yes, there is a 'higher calling' that purports that you can overcome in spite of the systematic bias that attempts to emasculate your self

---

[26] Ephesians 3:20; P.951 (NASB)
[27] Galatians 6:9-10; P.949 (NASB)

worth as a man. We, black Christian men, must 'be faithful even until death'; and the Lord Jesus will, 'in due season' deliver us from the evil that does beset us. We must again embrace the worthwhile attributes of hard work, love and respect for one another; because until we respect ourselves, no one else will respect us. Then the witness of our 'higher calling' will be reverberated throughout the annals of the halls of prejudice, injustice, and racism. A 'higher calling' that shouts out to the world, that I may not be able to dunk a basketball like an NBA pro, but I am a man; I may not be able to sing like Mr. Legend, but I am a man; I may not be able run as fast as the 'Usain Bolt', but I am still a man; and surely I am not as erudite as Neil deGrasse Tyson; but I am still a man; I may never be a President as Barack Obama, but I am still a man; I am a man because I accept my 'higher calling' to be responsible for my actions, and my shortcomings; recognizing that I have been the catalyst of the problems in my life; and not the panacea that seeks to resolve the issues. The 'higher calling' is born out of a new sense of identity; in other words I know who I am, and "[28]But by the grace of God I am what I am", and His grace toward me did not prove vain; but I labored more than all of them, yet not I, but the grace of God with me."

When black men have no legitimate means available to pursue life, liberty, justice, and the American dream; they will seek an illegitimate one. Unfortunately, too many of our young black men have chosen the path of least resistance, and that is the 'drug economy' that openly thrives in primarily low income predominantly black and brown neighborhoods.There is, however, a gross misconception that the drug problem is a black and brown problem,but you do know that opioids, heroin, and higher cost designer drugs do not discriminate. The illegal drugs and the drug economy has, and is, affecting all racial and gender boundaries. The only basic peculiarity of this drug economy is that poor disenfranchised blacks and browns have embraced it as if it was the answer to their grandest dreams. All of a

---

[28] I Corinthians 15:10; P.936 (NASB)

sudden, he who had been excluded from the great American dream of affluence and materialism, can now be a consumer of the finer things of life. He has been recruited by the prejudicial circumstances of life from the day he was born, and enticed perpetually by circumstances beyond his control. The only example of success that he has ever seen was the drug dealer, because he was the only one that possessed the holy grail that was revered as success in his world; a lot of money, the prettiest and finest women, and the most expensive cars. It did not matter to him as to the order in which they were acquired, but since he had no other means of acquiring these; he took the only path that he felt was available to him. He tells himself that he can make a small fortune working in the drug economy, so he weighs the risk of what he stands to gain, against what he stands to lose in light of his present hopeless circumstances. So he says to himself, "I'll take a chance." He surmises that since he has nothing, and the system is rigged to insure his imprisonment, death or both. He says, "What do I have to lose?" If I do nothing, I will die right here, and in my present condition I never have lived. So he laments, "I'm already dead and there is nothing for me, but the process of suffering and dying slowly." He sees no escape and he eventually sells out to the drug economy. He soon becomes a go-fer, a pusher, a preparer, a supplier, and sometimes a user; and he seeks to climb the ranks of the chain of command, and maybe one day he will be a distributor long enough to make the one deal that will set him up for life, so he can retire and get out of the business wealthy. That is his dream, that is his plan. That is what they all think and believe at the onset of selling out to the drug culture. The reality is this, the only ones safe from persecution and violence are the lawyers, and the CDB's; the Chief Drugs Bosses. They are insulated by the lawyers, politicians, and law enforcement. If there is any legal threat coming their way, they merely feed some of the lower echelon personnel to the quasi-justice system, and the beat goes on. The real benefactors of the wealth of the drug economy remain incognito, and are rarely prosecuted when indicted or caught. Many of those in authoritative positions, in order to effectively curb the influx and use of drugs, are users of drugs; and/or benefactors of the cash flow generated by the drug economy. But as dismal and as dark as the way may appear, when it seems as though we have fallen as low as we can; and even in the [29]"Valley of Achor" (Valley of Trouble), if we listen with spiritual hearing, we hear a 'wee small voice' that is weeping and wailing for the young black men that have been sacrificed to the drug economy, that have been murdered by over zealous bigoted law enforcement officers, that have been imprisoned unjustly; but yet, through the great cloud of despair there is the sound of joy and gladness that reverberates through the annals of time and eternity that there is a light of hope that shines above the horizon and that hope is named Jesus, who is the Son of the Living God. Jesus will bring justice and judgment to this world, and we, as a people, will no longer endure the misery or disdain of the great Emasculation Proclamation.

It is an extremely disheartening state of affairs to observe the total dysfunction of the black family unit today. A poor self image of our men, mutual distrust between black men and women, black women that have the persona and position of a man as head of the house (many times out of necessity), lack of men in the home curries lesbianism and homosexuality, the drug economy and gang affiliation as a substitute for family; all of the aforementioned are the end result of the emasculation conspiracy of America. The black family unit has been completely discombobulated during the period of forced slavery, and the plantation spirit of slavery vexes the hearts and minds of the children of slavery to this very day. The plantation spirit of slavery that restricts us from lifting our eyes up in the dignity of who we can become; and causes us to focus and remain stagnant in 'our place'. The plantation spirit of stereotyping us as lazy, shiftless, ignorant, and incapable of moral acts of perpetuity, because we have been seen as chattel to be used at the discretion of the *'masters'*. The plantation spirit of slavery that

---

[29] Reference: Valley of Achor, Joshua 7:24; P.179 (NASB)

has sold our emasculated bodies, minds, and souls continually to the ungrateful desires of the *'master.'* The plantation spirit of slavery that disallowed the authority of the black male, and promoted the black woman as head of household; and used black women as an instrument of the white master's will and pleasure in inordinate sexual desires. The black female was employable, her man wasn't; she was not considered as a threat, but her man was. The black female was the pivotal factor that allowed the remnant to survive long enough to observe the vestige of freedom, though not attained; but yet visible. She was strong and courageous; and the glue that was a bond of love that reared, nurtured, and protected her children, and her husband in times past. BUT NOW the baton needs to be taken by the black man, and we must run the race that God has set before us, we must stretch toward the prize of the high calling of manhood, fatherhood, and being the leader of the family. This can only be accomplished by the power of the indwelling Holy Spirit, and the Lord Jesus Christ. We as black Christian men have been called to a 'higher calling', you see we have no equal in this world. We are God's chosen people, we are His royal priesthood, we are His holy nation, we are His peculiar people, and we are all of that, so that we might reveal to the world a reflection of Him that has brought us out of the darkness of slavery, and into His marvelous light of freedom. We were not chosen to be slaves; we were not chosen to be murderers; we were not chosen to be criminals, thieves, womanizers, slothful, hustlers, drug lords, pushers, addicts, rapist.or players; BUT we have been chosen because we have a destiny to fulfill, and though the world may have meant to do us harm, though they have conspired against us, though they sought to imprison and kill us; BUT GOD has sent us here to do a good work in His name. So my brothers and sisters do we choose death, or do we choose destiny? If it is death, then continue to die under the oppressive hand of the 'Emasculation Conspiracy'; but if it is destiny, then accept the challenge of the "higher calling" that is to be found in Christ Jesus our Lord. And when that day comes, and we have come to the end of our journey, then and only then can we sing, not 'shall'; but rather "WE Have Overcome Today, not someday. Then the anthem that we sing will ring and resound the truth of its word:

> [30]Lift every voice and sing,
> 'Till earth and heaven ring;
> Ring with the harmonies of liberty;
> Let our rejoicing rise,
> High as the listening skies,
> Let it resound loud as the rolling sea.
>
> Sing a song full of the faith
> That the dark past has taught us,
> Sing a song full of the hope
> That the present has brought us;
> Facing the rising sun
> Of a new day begun,
> Let us march on till VICTORY is won.

---

[30] Reference: "Lift Every Voice and Sing"; James Weldon Johnson, National Baptist Hymnal, #477

CHAPTER III

The Slippery Slope Hypothesis

Revelations 2:12-17: P.999 (NASB)

And to the angel of the church in Pergamum write: To the One who has the sharp two-edged Sword say this: "I know your works, and where you dwell, where Satan's throne is. And you hold fast to My name, and did not deny My faith even in the days in which Antipas was My faithful martyr, who was killed among you, where Satan dwells. But I have a few things against you, because you have there those who hold the doctrine of Balaam, who taught Balak to put a stumbling block before the children of Israel, to eat things sacrificed to idols, and to commit sexual immorality. Thus you also have those who hold the doctrine of the Nicolaitans, which things I hate. Repent; or else I will come to you quickly, and will fight against them with the word of My mouth. He who has an ear, let him hear what the Spirit says to the churches. To him who overcomes I will give some of the hidden manna to eat. And I will give him a white stone, and on the stone a new name written which no one knows except him who receives it."

Numbers 22:7-8;P.128 (NASB)
"So the elders of Moab and the Elders of Median departed with the diviner's fee in their hand, and they came to Balaam and spoke to him the words of Balak. And he said to them, Lodge here tonight, and I will bring back word to you, as the Lord speaks to me. So the princes of Moab stayed with Balaam."

+++Note: Though Balaam was a false prophet, he allows the prince of Balak to persuade him to defy the very God he purported to be serving.

Numbers 22:20-21;P.128 (NASB)
Hence: "And God came to Balaam at night and said to him, "If the men come to call you, rise and go with them, but only the word which I speak to you-that you shall do. So Balaam rose in the morning, saddled his donkey, and went with the princes of Moab."

PROLOGUE:

The church at Pergamum was guilty of allowing false doctrine and deceptive teachings to be espoused to the believers of the church by non-believers. In the passage above, Balaam was a false prophet that had access to God, but refused to be obedient in order to gain wealth. He had a faustian nature that overruled his spirituality and prophetic office; and as a consequence, his heart was corrupted by an inordinate desire for worldly gain. In his effort to adhere to the wishes of Balak the king of Moab to proclaim a curse on the children of

Israel; Balaam could only proclaim blessings upon the nation of Israel. Balaam was a hireling prophet that would eventually fall short of his Godly mission, and become a prophet of deception and disobedience, all because he loved money more than God. He would fall short of his call and the holiness of his office; and the instructions that God had given him. Notice in Numbers 22:20 and 21; God spoke to Balaam at night, and told him. that 'if the men come to him the next morning he could go with them, but speak only the words that God would speak to him.' If you read carefully, no men came to him the next morning; but Balaam rose up, saddled his donkey, and went with them! They did not come to him, he went to them. The irony of it all, is that after his experience with his rebellious talking donkey, Balaam could only bless the children of Israel, and not curse them. Balaam's sin was not what he prophesied, but the advice he gave Balak was to allow the women of Moab to intermarry with the men of Israel; and the Moabite women would entice the men of Israel to commit idolatry through their foreign wives. Balaam was a hireling prophet that could be bought by the highest bidder; but God's truth was retroactively paid for by the living 'Truth', Jesus the Christ on the cross at Calvary. Balaam gave advice to Balak in an attempt to by-pass the mandate that God had given him. The church at Pergamum had people that had infiltrated their midst with false doctrine that opposed the word of God. So there are people in the Christian churches to this day that counter the word of God with a message that is diametrically in opposition to "Thus says the Lord." Many of these 'Balaamites' attempt to introduce their will, rather than His will; so they seek to get their false doctrine to the membership by persuading the 'angel', the 'Pastors,' the 'teachers' to adhere to their self serving apostatic untruth. The end result of this act is that many 'angels', 'Pastors', and teachers have been receptive to this mis-direction approach, and it has resulted in "A Crisis in the Pulpit!"

The Slippery Slope Hypothesis

The angels, the Pastors of the churches of the 21st century will be confronted by the spiritual wickedness of Satan and his demonic influences in this current world order. There will be an ever increasing onslaught of Satan's heretical doctrines refuting the Holy Bible, which is the living Word of God. Satan's goal is to replace biblical doctrine with his humanistic, hedonistic, and materialistic doctrine of this world. The church at Pergamum was located in the capital city of Satan's domain, and was for the greater part, an obedient and faithful church. This church remained faithful to the Lord Jesus even in the midst of severe persecution by the enemies of Christ. During this time many were martyred, as aforementioned in verse 13; thousands were slaughtered because they refused to deny their faith in Jesus Christ as Lord and Savior. We need to recognize this Antipas, he is not the infamous King Herod Antipas, but this Antipas was a faithful follower of the Lord Jesus. There is no further mention of him, but he is worthy of mentioning because the Lord knew his name, and chose to [31]mention his sacrifice in His 'Revelations' to the world. It is also noteworthy that the church of Pergamum receives some praise from the Master, but He also admonishes them; He says, 'But I have a few things against you, because you have there those who hold the doctrine of Balaam, and put a stumbling block before the children of Israel, to eat things sacrificed to idols, and to commit sexual immorality and those who hold the doctrine of the Nicolaitans, which things I hate.' The Lord says, "Which things I hate!"

The very idea that God hates anything is repugnant to many Christians. I am reminded of Balaam, the hireling prophet, who prostituted his calling and gift for the wealth of this world. Balak was the king of Moab, and he sought to hire Balaam to place a curse on the nomadic children of Israel. The Israelites encamped on the border of the nation of Moab, and there was such a great number of them,

---

[31] Reference: Numbers 22-25; (NASB)

that Balak became fearful and refused to allow them permission to pass through their territory. Balak sends for this Balaam, hireling prophet, priest, and warlock; and offers him riches and wealth if he would curse the children of Israel. Balak was actually fighting a battle that he had already won, because [32]God had forbidden Israel from attacking Moab. It was a blessing that Balak did not know that he already had. How many of us are praying for a blessing that we already have, begging the Lord for what He has already given? When Balaam arrived at the scene to perform the curse only to find out that he could only prophecy what the Lord had placed in his heart and on his tongue. He said, [33]"How shall I curse whom God has not cursed?" When Balaam opens his mouth unto the Lord, he can only bless the children of Israel. Four times Balaam attempts to curse, but can only bless God's chosen. Balak became extremely agitated at Balaam because he wasn't cursing Israel, but continued to bless them. The sin of Balaam came not in his desire to serve and please the pagan king, Balak, but Balaam's sin was, in his inordinate desire to obtain wealth by any means. You see, Balaam gave some very detrimental and pertinent advice to Balak, that would have a long term effect on the monotheistic relationship between God and Israel. Balaam's greater sin was his counseling of Balak, advising Balaam to allow the idolatrous women of Moab to marry the men of Israel; by doing so, they would eventually turn their hearts to worship the false gods of Moab. The children of Israel would be breaking the very first commandment of the Mosaic Law. [34] "You shall have no other gods before Me." [35]" So Israel joined themselves to Baal of Peor, and the Lord was angry against Israel". What Balaam succeeded in accomplishing was the corruption of God's chosen people by creating a union between Balak's idolatrous religion, and the monotheistic calling of God to the children of Israel. In other

---

[32] Reference: Deuteronomy 2:1-9 (NASB)
[33] Numbers 23:8; P.129 (NASB)
[34] Exodus 20:3; P.60 (NASB)
[35] Numbers 25:3; P.131 (NASB)

words, Balak could destroy Israel for within, rather than without; and it could be accomplished by planting the seed of corruption internally in the guise of sexual immorality and false doctrine. Israel would be guilty of trying to blend worldly doctrine with the spiritual covenant the one true God had made with them through the Abrahamic Covenant. By attempting to mix the doctrine of the world with the covenant promises of God, they would render the original relationship null and void; and though the Abrahamic Covenant was unconditional, all the conditional promises and favor of the Lord would be of non-effect.

When the church attempts to supplant the Word of God with even an iota of the world's doctrine, then it has started an ongoing decline in the areas of morality, obedience, and peace. This is the first step in the process of introducing into the church a 'slippery slope' of degradation that will force the church to continue on a downward spiral into the arena of false doctrine and idolatry; and the doctrine of the Nicolaitans was another contributing factor that increased the dangers of the slippery slope hypothesis. The Nicolaitans were those in the church who practiced licentious living; they believed that since I am saved no matter what I do, then I can do whatever I want, including sin. So I can marry whom I please, I can commit sexual immoral acts, I am free from the penalty of sin, because I am saved regardless of any immoral conduct. Once the church rejects any of God's commandments as erroneous, and accepts the morality of the world as truth, then sin, and the Word of God will no longer be applicable. So you accept whatever the world decrees as the truth, and whatever deeds that are diametrically opposed to the Word of God of no effect. This is a snare of Satan that is designed to compel one to step out onto the slippery slope of sin. Satan attempts to entice the Pastors, the angels, of the church into validating sinful behavior as of non-effect to the church, and attempts to persuade its members that it is acceptable to God. The Nicolaitans wanted to sin overtly, and the church to be muzzled, to be silent; but not only that, they wanted to rewrite and reinterpret the Word of God to support their sinful living. That is the slippery slope on which the church finds itself today. Most Christians that fall into the category of being Balaamites; and/or Nicolaitans, are generally those who take the position that Christian morals are too restrictive. So they seek a loophole that will allow them to be comfortable in the sinful desires of their heart. The Balaamites and Nicolaitans are those Christians who seek a loophole that will allow them to be saved, and comfortable, as they engage in immoral acts of this world. They also want a Holy, Righteous God to accept and approve their sinfulness; so they, in order to try and justify their disobedience to the commandments of God revealed by His Holy Bible, seek to reinterpret the part of the word of God that condemns their particular sin or sins. In today's church we find these slippery slope church members are those who try to justify their acts of adultery, homosexuality, lesbianism, fornication, dishonesty, lying, abortions, drunkenness, stealing and iniquitous behaviors in general, by quoting what the world has mandated, rather than what God has commanded. It is rather as the former Mayor of New York City, Rudy Giuliani, stated, "the truth isn't truth." Once they have accepted the world's doctrine, as opposed to the Word of God; they have started sliding down the slippery slope of sin and degradation, and the decline of the downward slope increases with each sin. The more they sin, the more they slide down the slippery slope of sin.

INTERLUDE:

The Nicolaitans of this world want Christians to believe that sexual immorality; such as lesbianism, homosexuality, fornication, and adultery are just 'alternative lifestyles'; and that God's love is so great that He would never condemn those who love one another, no matter the gender. After all, God is Love, and didn't He say that we ought to love one another. Surely God is not a God that would exclude anyone because they loved someone of the same sex; after all it is love, isn't it? Yes, God loves because God is Love; but God is

Just, and He is a God of Wrath, [36]"For the wrath of God is revealed from heaven against all ungodliness and unrighteousness of men who suppress the truth in unrighteousness, because that which is known about God is evident within them; for God made it evident to them." The world's doctrine is that God's love is more than sufficient to include them without conviction or damnation. But what about God's Justice, Righteousness, and Holiness? What of His wrath against all ungodliness and unrighteousness, and what of His saying, "which such things I hate"? You say God cannot hate, well His disdain for the acts of sin is so great that physical death is the penalty for sin. [37]"The wages of sin is death,....."; and by the way, death is no friend of man; because it is an enemy of God and man. The Bible says, [38]"The last enemy that will be demolished is death." God hates sin and He proves it by revealing His disdain for it by the penalty that ensued after it. When one slides so far down the slippery slope of sin to a point that they can no longer recognize sin as sin; and begins to call right, wrong; and wrong, right; then there is no redemption available because there can be no conviction, no repentance, no remorse because sin is not recognized as sin.

While the angels, the pastors are silent and the world's decree is that [39]"it's your thing, do what you wanna do, I can't tell you who to... ... ...'; sounds familiar? This is the creed of many Christians; 'anything you want to do is okay with me, as long as it doesn't affect me'. The idea that the sins of others does not, and will not affect me, is prevalent throughout society and Christendom. Well it does have an impact on you, your children, grandchildren, brothers, sisters, and even parents and those of the world, both saved and unsaved. The world will concoct every defensive argument that it can muster to discredit the righteous demands of God. The world believes that truth is relevant, and that right or wrong is governed by

---

[36] Roman 1:18-19; P. 915 (NASB)
[37] Romans 6:23; P. 919 (NASB)
[38] I Corinthians 15:26; P. 936 (NASB)
[39] Reference: Song: "It's Your Thing"; The Isley Brothers, Motown-T-neck Label 1969

circumstance; and Satan's disciples publicize loud and clear what the world accepts as righteous, moral behavior, and will ostracize anyone that opposes them. Well the Word of God is immutable, the same yesterday, today and tomorrow. [40]Homosexuality is an abomination in the sight of God, and it is a sin; adultery is a sin; stealing is a sin, murder is a sin, fornication is a sin; sin is sin; SIN is anything, or all things, that trespasses against the will and the Word of God and His Righteousness. God is immutable and does not change His Truth or His mind. Truth is an absolute, and never abstract; there is no almost true, nearly true, just about true; it is either true, or it is false. Sin is sin, and to believe that the sins of others do not affect you, is to ignore the evidence that is contrary to that mind set. The whole world is affected by sin, and because the very earth itself cries out for deliverance from the corruptive effect of sin. Paul says., "...because the creation itself also will be delivered from the bondage of corruption into the glorious liberty of the children of God. For we know that the whole creation groans and labors with birth pangs together until now." All of creation seeks deliverance from the effects of bondage caused by our sins on Earth, and even in the universe. Sin affects all of God's creation, and only a cataclysmic intervention of the Almighty Mighty Jesus the Christ can overcome the penalty of sin, DEATH!!!

The Nicolaitans are also those in the church that have a philosophy steeped in hedonism as it relates to their lifestyle. They believe that the world was created for them, and they were made for the world; and life is all about living it up. It is all about eating, and drinking, and rising every day to play. You remember when the children of Israel were waiting at the base of Mt. Horeb, while Moses was in a holy conference with the Lord God at the top of the mountain. He was receiving the Ten Commandments that would set forth written precepts of religious and social conduct; but the children of Israel were breaking the laws before, during, and after they had been written and received by Moses. They grew tired of waiting on the man of

---

[40] Reference: Leviticus 20:13 & Romans 1:27 (NASB)

God, so they set up their own world government, and made a god that had not made them, but one that they had made; and the Bible says, [41]"and the people sat down to EAT, to DRINK, and rose up to PLAY."; and this is the philosophy of life that many, both saved and unsaved, have chosen. They were eating to create a corporate fellowship to sin; drinking to release them from an inner inhibition to sin; and playing was an outward show of their lack of shame! So, they had reached the bottom of the slippery slope of sin. No shame, no guilt, no conviction, no repentance, no man of God, no God, and that leaves only judgment. They did not appreciate their new found freedom because they did nothing to deserve or earn it. There was no reference to work; because the work had already been done by the Son of God, Jesus the Christ; so they had been freed from slavery by the grace and might of a loving God. This activity of the children of Israel began as a party; eating and drinking, but it developed into an orgy. The word 'play' as translated in some versions as 'revel', is thought to be an idiom for immoral sexual activity; and some theologians believe this is an indication of the influence of Canaanite culture of sex as a part of praising their gods. The Apostle Paul refers to this play as immoral sexual activity in the guise of worship, [42]" Do not become adulterers, as some of them were; as it is written, The people sat down to eat and drink, and stood up to play." Nor let us commit sexual immorality, as some of them did,...." The idea that it does not matter what sin I commit, so long as I repent is asinine; but the question is, why should God continue to forgive you for any sin that you know you are going to habitually commit repeatedly? Perhaps you forgot what is required in repentance. The Greek word, *metanoeo*, means 'to have another mind' or 'to change the mind', or 'to turn away from', or 'to do a 180 degree turn from sin, and turn toward God. If one has really repented, and their mind has changed, and they have turned away from sin; then to do another, and another, and another 180 degree and go backward; and have sin tightens its grip on you; well that ludicrous.

[41] Reference: Exodus 32:6; & I Corinthians 10:6-7 (NASB)

[42] Reference: I Corinthians 10:7 (NASB)

The continued practice and participation in sinful acts implies that you have never truly repented. You are in a slippery slope loop, caught between sin and foolishness, foolishness and sin; but have never truly repented of your sins. This is the worst slippery slope condition there is, because you are not even aware that you are trapped in a loop. When the Pastors, the angels, and Christendom refuse to confront their members and the world on the issue of overt sin; then they are of no value to the business of the Kingdom of God.

The slippery slope hypothesis is alive and well in the beginning of the 21st century, and those Christians, who have professed to believe, and know Christ as Lord and Savior, have avoided the ultimate purpose for the coming of the Lord Jesus; and that is to [43]"save His people from their sins." One of the paramount lessons that Jesus constantly revealed was the devastating effects that sin had rendered upon mankind, and the world. The slippery slope is a harrowing place to be, because when you go to that place, you become so focused on your sinful desires, that sin is no longer seen for what it truly is. Once you step onto the slippery slope it seems as if it is self-rewarding, because the more you give yourself to your desired sin, the less you see it as sin. When a person becomes desensitized to the point of not recognizing sin, and that person further rationalizes in their heart that if there is no such thing as sin; then I am not a sinner. If there is no sin, then they surmise they can do anything they want without repercussions; and at that place on the slippery slope salvation is no longer available, because there can be no conviction, there can be no salvation, and that my beloved is the bottom of the slippery slope. The ultimate aim of the slippery slope is to deposit your soul in HELL.

The conclusion of the slippery slope hypothesis is that of compromising God's Word so that one might attempt to justify their sins as of non-effect; and their sinful acts are not a contradiction to the mandates of the Holy God. Oh, my brothers and sisters, the reason the slope of sin is so slippery is because down through the ages of time, the

---

[43] Reference: Matthew 1:21 (NASB)

tears of those who have chosen the path of the slippery slope, rather than the way of the hope of God which is found in Christ Jesus. Tears that have been shed over eons of time, tears that have were filled with the corrupt agents of despair and hopelessness. Those agents have created moss and fungus by feeding on the constant nourishment of our deposits of sins in trying to justify our iniquities. Every time we attempt to compromise the Word of God, we add more tears, more moss, and we slide more and more down the slippery slope of sin; No, I'm not perfect, and yes I do sin sometimes, but sin will not reign over my life. I refuse to allow sin to have dominion over me, So, when I sin, I repent of that sin, and ask the Lord to forgive me, and I know He is faithful to forgive. I strive to overcome those sins that beset me, endeavoring to overcome sin before it becomes habitual. I give thanks and praise to God because I have victory over the slippery slope and sin by the power, grace, and atoning salvation given to me by my Lord and Savior, Jesus Christ.

CHAPTER IV

The Children of Jezebel: An Ungrateful Generation

Revelation 2:18-29;P.999 (NASB)
"And to the angel of the church in Thyatira write:
The Son of God, who has eyes like a flame of fire,
and His feet are like burnished bronze, says this:
'I know your deeds, and your love, and faith and
service and perseverance, and that your deeds of
late are greater than at first. But I have this against
you, that you tolerate the woman Jezebel, who calls
herself a prophetess, and she teaches and leads my
bond-servants astray so that they commit acts of
immorality and eat things sacrificed to idols. I gave
her time to repent, and she does not want to repent
of her immorality. Behold, I will throw her on a bed
of sickness, and those that commit adultery with
her into great tribulation, unless they repent of her
deeds. And I will kill her children with pestilence,
and all the churches will know that I am He who

searches the minds and hearts; and I will give to
each one of you according to your deeds. But I say
to you, the rest who are in Thyatira, who do not hold
this teaching, who have not known the deep things
of Satan, as they call them,I place no other burdens
on you. Nevertheless what you have, hold fast until
I come. He who overcomes, and he who keeps My
deeds until the end, to Him I will give authority over
the nations; and He shall rule them with a rod of iron,
as the vessels of the potter are broken to pieces, as I
also have received authority from My Father, and I
will give him the morning star. He who has an ear,
let him hear what the Spirit says to the churches.'"

II Kings: 9: 30-37; P. 307-308 (NASB)
"When Jehu came to Jezreel, Jezebel heard of it, and
she painted her eyes and adorned her head and looked
out the window. As Jehu entered the gate,she said,
"Is it well, Zimri, your master's Murderer?" Then he
lifted up his face to the window and said, "Who is on
my side? Who?" And two or three eunuchs looked
down at him. He said, "Throw her down." So they
threw her down, and some of her blood was sprinkled
on the wall and on the horses, and he trampled her
under foot. When he came in, he ate and drank; and
he said, "See now to this cursed woman and bury her;
for she is a king's daughter." They went to bury her,
but they found nothing more of her than the skull
and the feet and the palms of her hands. Therefore
they returned and told him. And he said, "This is
the word of the Lord,   which He spoke by His
servant Elijah the Tishbite, saying, 'In the property
of Jezreel the dogs shall eat the flesh of Jezebel; and

as dung on the face of the field in the property of Jezreel, so they cannot say,"This is Jezebel.""

PROLOGUE:

The 'Ballad of Jezebel' is still being sung with a distinct bravado that still resonates in many churches to this day. Many of the evangelical heralds of this day are echoing the sentiments of Jezebel. Jezebel is extremely persistent and forceful in her zest and zeal to obstruct the kingdom of God, and the message of the saving grace of my Lord and Savior Jesus the Christ. What is her message? What are her goals? What does she expect to gain? Jezebel's message is anti-Christ and anti-Christian; it is built on the concept of misinterpretation of the Word of God; and an erroneous application of the authority and the governance of the Church. Many Christian churches today are adhering to the heretical doctrine of Jezebel. Jezebel was a pagan queen of Israel, who influenced her impotent husband, King Ahab, to commit acts of idolatry and immorality. Some pastors are being influenced by allowing secular pundits to encourage their congregations to vote for the political party of their choice. They are bringing the world into the church, and the 'Ballad of Jezebel' has superseded the preaching of the gospel of Jesus the Christ. The marriage of the state and the church is a corrupt union that is diametrically in opposition to the will of God, the Word of God says, [44]"Or do you not know that your body is a temple of the Holy who is in you, whom you have from God, and that you are not your own." [45]"Just as God said, "I will dwell in them and walk among them; and I will be their God, and they shall be My people. Therefore, come out from their midst and be separate," says the Lord". And do not touch what is unclean; and I will welcome you. And I will be Father to you, and you shall be sons and daughters to Me," says the Lord Almighty. What shall be the defense of the

---

[44] I Corinthians 6:19; P.930 (NASB)
[45] II Corinthians 6:16b; P.941 (NASB)

Pastors, the angels of the Church when we go before the judgment seat of Christ? He will ask why did you allow the teachings of Jezebel to deceive you, and then you indoctrinated My people with her heretical teachings? What will be their reply to the great inquisition before the judgment seat of Christ? Many of these New Age Congregations have produced a new generation of church members that have missed the high calling of the Lord Jesus Christ, and the end of the matter is they are producing "The Children of Jezebel": and they are, "An Ungrateful Generation"!!!

The Children of Jezebel: An Ungrateful Generation

The Pastors, the angels, of the 21st century Christian churches must stand firm against the onslaught of Satan and his demonic spirits. There is no greater assault than the destructive manner in which Satan has utilized his powers of enticement and deceit to induce us to sacrifice our children as an offering to him. Many of our Christian Pastors and churches of this current generation have allowed, and even taught its members to engage in doctrinal intercourse with the seductively enticing teachings of Jezebel. Jezebel's teachings are enticing to all who will listen, but it's an even greater temptation to our children. The church, and the children are not the only ones affected by the doctrine of Jezebel; the world is accepting her teachings as well. The foundation of Jezebel's teachings are rooted and grounded in the doctrine of Satanism; and it expounds the Satanic message of humanism, materialism, and hedonism. When Pastors, and churches engage in doctrinal intercourse with the teachings of Jezebel; the church will bring forth children that will continue to propagate and birth an ever increasing multitude of children of Jezebel. Most Pastors and churches, and even the nation agonize over the sacrificial offering we have ceded to Satan and the demonic spirits of this world. We say we do not understand our children; we have no idea why they do the things they do; and what in the world is wrong with this generation? Have they gone completely crazy? Oh, this is a thankless, ungrateful generation; but we must recognize that most of them are children of Jezebel!

The children of Jezebel are everywhere, because they are our children; your children, and mine. They are the products of this world's system, and we have offered them as sacrifices to Satan in exchange for [46]'the kingdoms of this world'. In our zest and inordinate desire for the material status symbols of this world order, we have fallen for the wiles of Satan. Satan has deceived us into believing that happiness is to be attained in material wealth, and that good parents are obligated to obtain material wealth in order to bestow upon their children a multitude of material blessings that they do not need or deserve. We have allowed our children to fill the parental void of absentee parenting with the things of Jezebel. She was there when they needed a parent. She was wonderful, amazing, exciting, pleasing, permissive, alluring and accessible; and she acted as though she cared. She was exceedingly more attractive than our parents or the church. While we parents were busy working 24/7 to obtain material wealth and social status in humanistic pursuits, and aggressively seeking the pleasures of hedonistic activities; Jezebel was entertaining our children surreptitiously. Jezebel is alive and well, and the evidence of her doctrine is found in what she has bequeath to the world, to us and our children; she has left her <u>head, her feet, and her hands.</u>

Jezebel is Satan's seductive ambassador of death and her children usually die prematurely; and as the death toll mounts, most parents are not cognizant of the Jezebel syndrome. We seem to be helplessly paralyzed observers, as this generation of our children engage in annihilating themself in the endeavors of the<u> head, the feet, and the hands of Jezebel.</u> We parents have failed miserably because our children needed us, and not more stuff. We have failed as parents and Christians because we have not refuted the teachings of Jezebel. We

---

[46] Reference: Matthew 4:8 (NASB)

refuse to confront Jezebel because we feel powerless to confront the authority of this world's systemic Jezebelian authority. But we bear the name, Christians, because we belong to One [47]"Who is able to do far more abundantly beyond all that we ask or think, according to the power that works within us." The power that works within us is the indwelling Holy Spirit; and it is by the Holy Spirit we must confront the head, the feet, and the hands of Jezebel.

Some might ask, what is the significance of the hands, the feet, and the hands of Jezebel? We find the Jezebel narrative begins in the book of I Kings, Chapter 16, verse 31; but we will primarily focus on the demise of Jezebel in II Kings, Chapter 9, verse 30- 37. We remember how she persecuted the prophets; plundered and stole the vineyard of Naboth and killed him; pursued and attempted to kill Elijah; influenced and misguided her weak husband, King Ahab. She was also instrumental in encouraging the practice of idolatrous worship among the Israelites. Yes, she was a wicked force of evil whose objective was to turn the hearts of God's people to worship idols. She was an evil vengeful woman, but Elijah prophesied a fitting demise for this wicked queen. Elijah, the prophet of God, prophesied that,[48]"the dogs shall eat Jezebel by the wall of Jezreel." The culmination of that prophecy comes to fruition when Jehu, having executed the kings of Israel and Judah, rode into the town of Jezreel, and Jezebel heard that he was on his way. She arose and put on her makeup, perhaps in the hope of enticing him, but then she yelled out of an upstairs window an insult at Jehu. She calls him a 'murderer of his masters'. Needless to say, Jehu was not impressed. He called to the eunuchs that attended the queen, 'if there be any on my side, then throw her out of the upstairs window'. So the eunuchs cast her down to Jehu, who trampled her with the hooves of his horse, and dispatched her there forthwith. Later after he had eaten and rested, he ordered that her body be retrieved and buried, for he reasoned, she was after all 'the daughter of a king.' When his men went to the place where her

---

[47] Ephesians 3:20; P.951 (NASB)
[48] I Kings 21:23; P.296 (NASB)

body had been abandoned, much to their surprise, they found only her skull, her feet, and the palms of her hands; her head, her feet, and her hands. I would like to submit for your consideration that the remains of Jezebel are evident today, and they are alive and still influencing the church and society today. The head of Jezebel is leading our children down the path of unrighteousness and death; the hands of Jezebel are willingly offering our children as a sacrifice to Satan; and the feet of Jezebel are propagating the spirit of Satan to future generations.

The head of Jezebel is leading our children down the path of unrighteousness and death. Her head is the ultimate source of the doctrine of Jezebel. The head is where the brain, the mind, the thinking if initiated, and the philosophy of life is conceived. It is where 'the good, the bad, and the ugly' originates and resides. Jezebel has devised, through her false teaching, justification for our children to worship the idols of this world, rather than the God of all worlds. She has persuaded our children, this ungrateful generation, that materialism is the way to happiness; and that you must have the biggest, the best, and the latest stuff to be happy. The greatest contributor to this false doctrine is the vocal and visual exploitation of television, cell phones, social media, and the world wide WEB. This ungrateful generation has been constantly bombarded since birth with the message that to be cool, to be in vogue, to be in, accepted into the in-crowd; you must drive a certain high end car, wear only designer clothes, expensive tennis shoes, special haircuts and hairstyles, manicured fingernails, tattoos, designer manicures, and socialize only with a certain class of people; and most assuredly you must talk and walk in a manner acceptable to your new found status in this ungrateful generation. This ungrateful generation loves the things, the stuff more that they love their parents, family, or God.. They worship the created, rather than the Creator. They will never find happiness in things, because the things that are in demand today will not be in demand tomorrow. It's in-today, but gone tomorrow; a mirage of no lasting substance. The Pastors and angels of the church must preach that the only lasting joy or happiness will never be found in the things of this world; but

It can only be found in the immutability of the Creator of all that is. Jesus Christ is the same, yesterday, today, and forever, and in Him there is no change. If you are in with Jesus, you will be in forever; but if you are out of Jesus, you can come in-to Him. The children of this generation have been bombarded by the teachings of Jezebel, and their parents are just as materialistic; and many churches also echo the tenets of Jezebel. The parents of this ungrateful generation have been competing against the 'Jones', and their friends; the Pastors and churches vie against other Pastors and churches. How many members do you have? How large is your sanctuary? Is it carpeted with cushioned seats? Do you have an organ with a synthesizer? How is the air conditioning? What about online offerings and online streaming? The church has also adopted the teachings of the head of Jezebel, and it is the doctrine of 'thingalism'. This ungrateful generation has inherited 'thingalism' from their parents and the world; and they will not relinquish it without a fight. We, the parents and children are reaping the penalty of our lack of nurturing, lack of discipline, and lack of spending personal time with them in their formative years; and granting unconditional, and conditional love and support to them as parents, not as a friend. While we were working five days a week, and all the overtime that was offered; so that we could buy things for our family and children, because we did not want them to suffer from poverty and want, as many of us had been exposed to in our youth. So Jezebel interceded into their lives, and accepted the role of parenting that we had abandoned for the things of this world. She adopted our children and taught them what to worship, obey, and love; and she has given birth to this current ungrateful generation.

This ungrateful generation has no bearings or moral compass; no direction or morality. It is the 'what will be, let it be' generation; 'get what you can, any way you can'. They have been taught that it doesn't matter how you get it, as long as you get it. It doesn't matter if I disrespect my parents and others that love me. It doesn't matter if I place more credence in my friends than in my father and mother who provide me with the necessities of life; food, shelter, and some 'things'.

It doesn't matter if I am ungrateful, after all, Jezebel still loves me. Jezebel says that if I need someone to love me unconditionally, then I should become an unwed teenage mother, surely I can rear a child to love me. She teaches that true love must be expressed physically, and you must experience all kinds of physical love by being promiscuous. Jezebel teaches that since I feel that my parents and family have failed me, join a gang and they will be my new family; but remember you must kill to be initiated, but don't worry your new gang family will love you 'TO DEATH.' Jezebel teaches you that your parents don't really love you; and all you have to do is just pick up your cell phone and call her, she whispers seductively, "I love you and I am always near." The head of Jezebel is alive and well, and it is teaching our children to rebel against all that is good and Godly, and we ponder as parents, why this is an ungrateful generation.

Then there are the hands of Jezebel that are willingly offering our children as a sacrifice to Satan who is leading them to hell and death. Our young boys and men are being enticed by the hands of Jezebel that holds forth promises of money, girls, and status. If you sell drugs for the gang, then you will have money, and the girls will seek you, and you will be recognized as somebody. Jezebel's hands conceal the real cost for the things that she offers. When the palms of her hands face upward, she is tempting you with the promises of all that a young foolish male desires; but when her palms face downward; they hide the utter destruction and death that is the just reward for accepting what she is offering. Her hands force them to have a false sense of grandeur, steeped in the pride of life; desiring the stuff of this world, the lust of the eyes; and oh, sure she offers the clothes, the cars, the women, the lust of the eyes. Death and Hell is all that lies in the hands of Jezebel. Her hands are strangling the life out of our children and leading them down the road from whence there is no return. She makes promises that are fleeting away as fast as they come, she says, "With these hands I will give you gold, diamonds, pearls; with these hands I will give you fine expensive apparel; with these hands I will give you chariots of gold and silver; with these hands I will give you the desires of your heart; with these hands I will give you authority over men; and with these hands I will give you an early grave. The hands of Jezebel are alive and well, and they are evident in the continued destruction of this ungrateful generation.

Jezebel's _hands_ are symbolic of the deeds of indignation and degradation that have been issued from this ungrateful generation. This ungrateful generation is disrespectful and ungrateful, because we, the parents, schools, and churches have failed in the hands-on application of early discipline. We failed to have a hands-on relationship of authority when it was needed; as it related to respect, manners, and rewards bestowed on our children. Respect and manners begin in the home, and you nurture good behavior by rewarding good behavior, and obedience is taught by observation, and instruction in righteousness. Hands-on must be applied at an early age when it's appropo'. When the child does what is good and acceptable, the hands-on with a kiss and a hug; but when that child is consistently and intentionally disobedient, then you need to put some hands-on that butt. This ungrateful generation has never had fear or respect for parents or authority figures; such as, Pastors, policemen, teachers, and all who are legitimately in positions of authority for the common good. It is a process that should have begun from birth, because much of what a child becomes, is about that in which a child is exposed in their formative years. If the father and mother have respect for one another, it is the first relationship of respect that a child will witness. You cannot rear your child by a book written by a child psychiatrist, because there are no norms that are compatible with all children. What works for one or even 20, may not be applicable to all. You can talk to some children and they will comply; and some you can apply hands-on the butt; and they might still be disobedient; and if all else fails you have only one other course, call on Jesus to exercise that demon from your child (just a pun). You should call on the Lord Jesus before birth, after birth, and during the life of your child. The norm of the day is that corporal punishment is the wrong means of disciplining your child. Well, it is not the only solution, but it is one of the effective solutions. I will listen to my child but in the final decision, he or she has no vote, no authority; the authority is mine as the adult, the leader, provider, and spiritual guide of the family. There is nothing wrong with the hands-on approach when needed, The Bible says, [49]"Do not hold back discipline from the child; although you strike him with the rod, he will not die.", and "The rod and reproof give wisdom, but the child that gets his own way brings shame on his mother.", and "Train a child in the way he should go, and when he is old he will not depart from it." The most pivotal Scripture concerning this issue is directed at children, [50]"Honor (respect) your father and your mother, that your days may be prolonged in the land which the Lord your God gives you." This is the only commandment given with a direct promise. Save your child from the hands of Jezebel and lead them to the Lord Jesus and a long life in the land. Jesus will paralyze the hands of Jezebel and render them of no effect; and will turn this ungrateful generation into grateful believers in Christ Jesus our Lord.

Oh Lord, we have the <u>feet</u> of Jezebel that are propagating the spirit of Satan to future generations. It is a spirit that is diametrically opposed to the Gospel of Jesus Christ, which is the good news of the redemptive, salvific, atoning grace and sacrifice of the Savior, Jesus the Christ. Jezebel's feet spread the surreptitious news of a promise built on the foundation of a deceptive mirage of smoke and mirrors. Jezebel's feet are symbolic of the permeating impact that her false teaching has, and is having, on this ungrateful generation. She has feet active in social media, cell phones, gang affiliations, entertainment, schools, government, churches and homes: the effect of Jezebel's feet are everywhere. She has an open invitation to our child to try drugs, sex, and violence; she has convinced a multitude of the ungrateful generation to try any and everything. She tells them that 'everybody is doing it'; so it must be alright. Many of this generation pursue the feet of Jezebel as they lead them down the path of sin and death. Jezebel adopts those who lack responsible parenting, and soon they become

---

[49] Proverbs 22:6; 23:13; 29:15; P.533- 534 & 540, respectively (NASB)
[50] Exodus 20:12; P.60 (NASB)

disciples of Jezebel, and expand exponentially the corrupt message of Jezebel. Jezebel doesn't allow her prey to perceive the reality of her persona; so, [51] "she painted her eyes and adorned her head"; she put on her make-up and adorned her hair so that she might create the illusion of royalty, but there was an evil sadistic person behind a mask of deceit. Jezebel's adopted children aspire to be what she has exposed them to become; ungrateful children of the world.

INTERLUDE:

If I were an alien observing the earth from space, and had the ability to tune-in to the visual media what might I surmise? What would be my initial impression of the spectacle of television? I would first surmise that there are many hues and shapes to those entities shown, and that there seemed to be a sexual distinction by most, but not all. After a short period of scanning the various presentations, I would probably surmise that all of the darker shades of the entities have a certain function and all of the paler shades have another, there are scattered isolated exceptions. The darker ones seem to be having fun because, for the most part, all they do is sing, dance, play games, laugh, and be laughed at by the paler ones. The paler ones seem so serious; they kiss, make love, war, cry, eat, and laugh at the darker ones. Then I noticed that there is a larger group who are neither pale nor dark, but fall somewhere in the middle, there seems to be no real distinctive difference, so you see them on all stations. The pale ones and the lighter of the dark seem to be in charge of everything. As an alien I would come to a conclusion that it is amazing, that with all of the various divisions between these entities; how have they survived?

This ungrateful generation is ungrateful because they have not been told; or they have forgotten the many feet that have been sacrificed in times past, so that they might have the opportunity to overcome. The feet of Frederick Douglass, W. E. B. Du Bois,

---

[51] II Kings 9:30; P.307 (NASB)

George Washington Carver, Sojourner Truth, Mary B. McCloud, Dr. Ralph Bunche, Roy Wilkerson, Justice Thurgood Marshall, Ralph Abernathy, Congressman Adam C. Powell, Medgar Evers, Doctor Martin Luther King, Jr. and a multitude of others who will never be known. The feet of those that survived the past inhumane eras of; slave ships, slavery, persecution, Jim Crowism, 'separate but unequal facilities, segregation, economic suppression, ghettos, and past and present day police brutality, aggression, and murders; it's a perpetual battle, and the word is 'we still shall overcome' the feet Jezebel. Those feet that tread the path before us, and tread the rows of horrendous labor of cotton fields; feet that were baked by the searing blazingly hot sun of days of yore; feet that suffered the indignity of the slave master's whip: tired feet, degraded feet, sore feet, blistered feet, unhappy feet, crying feet, filthy feet, smelly feet, and even dying feet-feet that died horribly, excruciatingly painful feet so that this ungrateful generation might have an opportunity to mature and be grateful.

What shall I surmise from the preceding diatribe, thanks be to the Lord Jesus who did not leave us vulnerable and powerless. He gave us a method, a modus operandi (MO), so that we may resist and destroy the hands, the head, and the feet of Jezebel. The method is by the power of the indwelling Holy Spirit infused by prayer and the Word of God. We must continue to remind this ungrateful generation of the atoning grace of Jesus Christ, our Lord. The method is that through Christ we are recipients of a moral value system, undergirded by His power; that will allow us to reclaim our ungrateful children, and the dignity of their humanity and worth. Jesus was always about people being a priority over property. We, as parents, must recognize that our children must take precedence over our desires for the things of this world. We must do without many of the things, and other time consuming personal activities; and invest in a greater spiritual relationship with our children. It is not more things and money that they desire and need, it's more of Jesus and you that is needed. You do know that you[52] "can do all things through Christ which strengthens you"; and the [53]'battle is not yours, it is the Lord's'! Stop trying to combat Jezebel alone, take the Lord Jesus to the front lines with you. There is a war in progress and we [54]'fight against spiritual wickedness in high places, and the rulers of darkness of this world'; we cannot fight this war alone, we need the greatest weapon against evil given by God to the world, and that is Jesus Christ the Lord. The Lord has promised us that if we would[55] 'acknowledge Him, He will direct our path', and if you belong to Him, He has promised that he[56] 'will never forsake you, nor will I ever leave you'. We must fight the influence of Jezebel and save this ungrateful generation; because we love them and they belong to us, and not Jezebel.

Finally, we have the method to defeat head of Jezebel, which is Christ Jesus our Lord; we have the means to defeat the hands of Jezebel, by the power of the indwelling Holy spirit; and we have the mode to overcome the feet of Jezebel, by the evangelical outreach of the Pastors, the angels of the churches. Jesus is the method, the Holy Spirit is the means, and the called saints of God are the mode. We, as parents, are compelled to remove the stigma and stain of the doctrine of Jezebel from the presence of this ungrateful generation, so that they become all that God intended, and become a grateful generation. (AMEN)

---

[52] Reference: Philippians 4:13 (NASB)
[53] Reference: I Samuel 17:47 (NASB)
[54] Reference: Ephesians 6:12 (NASB)
[55] Reference: Proverbs 3:6 (NASB)
[56] Reference: Hebrews 13: 5; (NASB)

CHAPTER V

A Dead Church: A Drug Culture

Revelation 3:1-6;P.999 (NASB)

"And to the angel of the church in Sardis write: He who has the seven Spirits of God and the seven stars, says this:'I know your deeds, that you have a name that you are alive,but <u>you are dead</u>. <u>Wake up</u>, and strengthen the things that remain, which were about to die; for I have not found your deeds completed in the sight of my God. So remember what you have received and heard; and keep it, and repent. Therefore if you do not <u>wake up</u>, I will come like a thief, and you will not know at what hour I will come to you. But you have a few people in Sardis who have not soiled their garments;and they will walk with me in white, for they are worthy. He who overcomes will thus be clothed in white garments; and I will not erase his name from the book of life, and I will confess his name before My Father and before His

angels. He who has an ear, let Him hear what the
Spirit says to the churches'

PROLOGUE:

The neo-modern day Christian Church is approaching a critical impasse as it relates to its call and mission in this 21st century culture. The New Age Christian Church transitioned from the evangelical mission mandated by the Lord Jesus when He submitted the charge to all churches that bear the name, Christian: [57]"Go therefore and make disciples of all nations, baptizing them in the name of the Father, and the Son, and the Holy Spirit, teaching them to observe all that I have commanded you; and Lo, I am with you always, even to the end of the age."This mandate was given to every called, saved member of the body of Christ; and it renders all saved christians to focus on presenting the gospel of Christ to the world. It appears that many of the mega-churches have gained a multitude of people, but have fallen asleep on saving souls. So many of these new age mega-churches have become more of a Sunday morning social gathering, than a spiritual praise and worship of the Master, Jesus the Christ! Many have fallen asleep, and no longer focus on preaching for conviction and repentance; but their focus is on the presentation of scripted preaching and entertainment that is devoid of the presence of the Spirit of Christ Jesus. If the Christian Church doesn't awaken; the Lord will call us, and all church leaders that are asleep, to be accountable for our failure to obey His call to serve and obey. WAKE UP!!!

A Dead Church: A Drug Culture

There have been four cataclysmic events in modern historical annals that have had a holocaustic effect upon an entire race of people;

---

[57] Matthew 28:19-20;P.815 (NASB)

and three of those four have been paramount in the history of America. The first was the genocidal effect of the eradication of the only true native Americans, the American indians; second was the horrific enslavement and mistreatment of men primarily of African origin, and the continued disenfranchisement of the same; the third event did not occur in America, but was also a racist attempt at complete genocide of an entire race of people; it was Nazi Germany, or the German Reich under the infamous tyrant, Adolf Hitler; who sought to eliminate Jews from Eastern Europe and eventually the world. It is frequently referred to as, 'the Holocaust'; and the fourth event is the destruction and devastation that illegal drugs and the 'drug culture' has had, and is having, upon the people of this great nation, America. Nothing in recent history has so devastated the social order of communities as has the advent of the drug culture. The communities that have been affected disproportionately are those of low income predominantly black and brown communities. The black communities of America, by the grace of God, have overcome the night riding cowardice acts of hangings, arsons, rapes and intimidation of the Klu klux Klan, and a racist national agenda to spread fear, hopelessness, and despair.; and by the grace of God, we have overcome most of the barriers of the Jim Crow era of separate and unequal system of politics, religion, economics, and society; but Satan now seeks to destroy us, not only by the KKK, and a multitude of other white extremist groups, but by the three C's, 'Crack, Crank, Cocaine.

Considering the impact that the drug culture has had, and is having on communities of color; it appears that the Christian church has fallen asleep; and yes, is apparently dead to this death dealing blow that has; and is, being perpetuated in predominantly black and brown communities. There has been an onslaught of issues that have confronted the truths of God's love letter to all, the Bible. It is written to His children, the world; and while we confront the issues of abortion, homosexuality, pornography, social injustice, and police murdering black men; there has been an attempt by the world to politicize these issues that are primarily indicative of a morally bankrupt society. They are, for the Christian; however, moral issues that are addressed and governed by the Word of God. If God said no to a sinful act in the past, then it is still a sin, and will ever be; because God is immutable, and so are His commandments. He does not change His mind, "[58] Jesus Christ is the same yesterday, today, and tomorrow." When we accept the immorality of the world as greater than the righteous mandates of God, then we are indicting God as a liar; and that His Word, the Holy Bible is erroneous. If you choose the world's immorality because it agrees with your sinful acts or deeds that you chose to perform or accept; it does not change the fact that it is still a sin according to the Word of God. Whether you are pro, or con with the world's morality has no bearing as far as 'thus says the Lord'; the customs and mores of the world can never supersede the Will, the Way, and the Word of God; His word has been established in eternity and does not change. God has spoken, [59] "So will my word be which goes forth from My mouth; it will not return to Me empty, without accomplishing what I desire, and without succeeding in the matter for which I sent it". So the Lord God issues an indictment against the church that by reputation it is alive, but in fact it is dead; and the Lord says something profound, and disturbing to the church at Sardis and to the Christian church today, WAKE UP! Oh, my brothers and sisters, it is sad testimony when we, the church, are dead asleep while the Master has need of us. Consider that when Jesus was in the garden at the mount of Olives, the disciples were asleep as He prayed concerning the [60]'cup' that He was to endure; and He asked a pertinent, but soul searching question, [61]"So you men could not keep watch with Me for one hour?" The question is, are we betraying the Lord Jesus at a critical time in the history of our nation, our world? The Lord is saying to His church, WAKE UP!

---

[58] Hebrews 13:8; P.982 (NASB)
[59] Isaiah 55:11; P.602 (NASB)
[60] Reference: Matthew 26:40 (NASB)
[61] Matthew 26:43;P.812 (NASB)

The drug culture and economy has so permeated our society that law enforcement agencies, courts, and prisons are completely inundated with offenders and convicts. We, Christians, love to recite the 23rd Psalms when we find ourselves in dire trials and tribulations. We pray earnestly for the Lord to intervene and deliver us from the burden of what we have reaped; the fruit of what we have sown, or the lack of sowing any good. We have turned our backs on the problems of our drug infested communities, and ignored the resulting devastation of the assault of Satanic forces on our youth and especially young men of color. Yes, we laud the 23rd psalm, "The Lord is my shepherd", and we are vehement and resolute in that prayer. The addict; however, the user of drugs, is also deeply entrenched in his addiction; so much so, that they have substituted drugs for God with their habitual addiction in an attempt to escape from the reality of life, only to descend into the tormenting illusional depths of hell and unfulfilled desires. Instead of the 23rd Psalm, a young black drug addict residing in New York's Harlem community wrote his own parody to the 23rd Psalm:

> [62]"Cocaine is my shepherd, I shall not want.
> It maketh me to lie down in gutters,
> It leadeth me beside still madness,
> It destroys my soul.
> It leadeth me in the paths of hell for its
> namesake.
> Yea, though I walk through the valley
> of the shadow of death,
> I will fear no evil, for crack is with me.
> my syringe and needle shall comfort me.
> Thou puttest me to shame in the presence
> of mine enemies.
> Thou anointest my head with madness;
> my cup runneth over with sorrow.

---

[62] Reference: Collins, Harper/ Fontana Books/London, England; author:anon, 1965, p.163

Surely hate and evil shall follow me
all the days of my life,
And I will dwell in the house of misery
and disgrace forever."

What a talent this young man possessed, a gift that possibly could have contributed to the arts of society, but has long been lost to the disease that is running rampant in America, and yea, even the world. I suggest to you that where there is a disease, the Lord has a cure. First let us diagnose the disease, and then issue a prognosis, and then propose a cure.

THE DIAGNOSIS

The disease is drug addiction, and the perpetrators of it; the users, the pusher, the suppliers, the producers and the benefactors. It is a disease of epic proportions in black communities; and it is having a genocidal effect on a whole generation of young minority males. The drug culture is an economic system within itself. The amount of currency being generated by illegal drugs in America is 'mind boggling'; and the real benefactors of the currency being generated aren't black or brown males alone, most are merely pawns for those who 'sit in high places'; who are insulated from any hands on involvement, and when exposed they merely buy their way out of any difficulties that come their way. They are usually wealthy men with positions and power in their communities. They are the new 'untouchables' because so many of the higher authorities that have the responsibility of seeking systemic eradication and justice, are themselves users, and are receiving 'filthy lucre'. They are the perpetrators of [63]"spiritual wickedness in high places", being controlled by the [64]"rulers of the darkness of this world." They are men usually of a good reputation in

---

[63] Reference: Ephesians 6:12; P.953 (NASB)
[64] Ibidem

their communities; but choose not to be cognizant of the communities, and the young lives they are instrumental in destroying. Some attend church, probably one of the dead churches, where they sometimes contribute abundantly to the church, donate liberally to charities, support politicians, especially those that are of no effect to their illegal criminal activities. They also bribe law enforcement to look away from the drug activity in the communities, and pay a 12 or 13 year old $200- $1000 a week to sell [65]'white death' in his community. This 12 or 13 year old child, who has nothing, knows nothing, sees no way out of their cycle of despair and poverty makes a choice between a $7.50 an hour job at McDonalds or Burger King; or $300.00 a week or more pushing dope for the man. He has observed those in the community that have tried to adhere to the system; only to have their dreams and aspirations derailed by the many roadblocks that skin color and heritage forces them to overcome to be successful. So this young black or brown boy has said to an America that has excluded him from the mainstream of economic success, "I will create my own economic system even if it kills me, I have nothing, what do I have to lose?" He is not blind to the fact that he probably won't live long enough to enjoy his newfound wealth, but then he has considered the alternatives; and he contends that death in the streets with money is far better than death in the ghetto with no money. If a rival gang doesn't kill him, then a policeman will, so when he finally grows tired of having nothing, he decides to rob the corner liquor store out of desperation; or he joins the mainstream of economic 'SUCCESS' in the black community; he becomes a pusher at the ripe old street age of 13 and becomes 'DEAD' or in PRISON by 18. It is a sad state of affairs that America has not realized that the drug culture is not discriminatory; it has graduated since the 70's and 80's into an Opioid epidemic that is rampant in the white middle class America also. Drugs are a contagious disease that knows no skin color, no religion, no economic class, and has no mercy. It has no shame, compassion, no conscience, no pity, and is loveless.

---

[65] Definition: Colloquial street terminology synonymously used to refer to Cocaine.

It is the chief perpetrator of murders, robberies, prostitution, rape, divorce, gambling, incest and child abuse in America. It is a disease that we as a nation refuse to confront seriously with a determined national resolve. The diagnosis is dire and currently there is no light to be seen, not even a glimmer; and the church must Wake Up!!!

THE PROGNOSIS

While the church is dead or asleep, the prognosis is, as it relates to the drug culture of America, dire. The use and misuse of drugs, legal and illegal, is at a lethal, epidemic proportions in America; and no person, persons, or group is able to stem the onslaught of the drug culture. It is not a priority of the powers of law enforcement and the government, because it would affect the economy, personally and nationally. The pharmaceutical industry spends great amounts of money to hinder any reforms that would affect price gouging or distribution of their products, both the legal and illegal sales. In Mexico you can buy the same brand drugs at a fourth of the price that they cost in America; and you can purchase most of them across the counter at the local market place without a prescription. You can go online and order the same prescription drugs from Canada at a third to fifty percent of what they cost in America. Those who are in authority, who we voted into office, do nothing because the majority of the contributors to their re-elections are the CEO's, and major corporations, pharmaceutical industries; and like the NRA, they care nothing about the lethal toll that their product is having in all communities of America; but disproportionately greater in black and brown communities. They are only concerned about profit and maintaining the status quo, even when their own loved ones have also surrendered to the deadly whims of the drug culture. We need to WAKE UP church!

Why did the communities so eagerly accept this grotesque monster, the drug culture? There are three questions that we shall address for a greater understanding of the future course and impact of the dilemma we now confront.

1. Why was this 'chimera' so eagerly received in the minority communities?
2. What was different about that generation, and this current generation that made them fertile ground to receive this seed of corruption and death?
3. Why did the local community churches fail in their calling to stand in the gap and defend the helpless?

WHY WAS THIS [66]'CHIMERA' SO EAGERLY RECEIVED IN THE MINORITY COMMUNITIES?

One of the primary reasons was the limited number of avenues of escape from an ever recurring cycle of poverty and systemic discrimination. It was accepted as a means to confront 'white America' in terms that they would readily understand, 'money honey'. The minorities, primarily males of their communities, saw money as power; because in America, money is power. So those who acquiesced to the drug economy, suffered from a self imposed blindness to the consequences that would be heaped on their communities, its people, and themselves. It was the money and all that it offered, and not the negative impact that the drugs would have on so many of the very people they loved. Young minority men became an endangered species, and prison and death became the norm as the drug culture ushered in the 21st century. They surmised that if there is a high probability that they will never reach the age of 21; and if they have a choice between dying penniless, and dying with means to purchase the 'stuff' of life; far too many chose to embrace the 'drug economy'. Dying poor and penniless was a slow agonizing death; but with the money they could

---

[66] Definition: Chimera-a horrible or unreal monster of mythology; so dreadful as to be literally unreal.

earn working for 'the man' in the drug economy, they could at least live high and mighty once before they die; after all, the only successful people with whom they could identify within their community was the preacher, the teachers, the pimps, and dope dealers. They were tired of being exposed to all of the exorbitant materialism displayed on TV, only to see it, and never have it; it created a heart of envy and despair. They felt like a drowning man going down for the third time; so like a drowning man, they began to grope for anything that would allow them to escape from their cycle of existence and death.

WHAT WAS DIFFERENT ABOUT THIS CURRENT GENERATION?

If you have noticed, I have been using the word 'community' to refer to the abode, culture, and social environment; and the relationships into which many minorities are born. It is a misnomer to use the word community, in the sense of 'coming together as one viable entity'; surely that is non-existent in most minority communities today. The only unity that exists now is that which comes from a common interest; such as, the church which has its followers, the sports groups that have its followers, the hustlers and pimps, that have their followers, and the pushers and users; and each group has its own agenda. All are considered the new enterprises, the new businesses, the new economy; if you want money and success in the community, then you must be pursuing with great vigor one of these lofty enterprises. The greatest difference that this generation faces is there is no significant family structure to support and discipline the children, because this generation is being conceived and reared by an undisciplined generation. This generation has no parental discipline or respect because their daddies and mommies have none, and you cannot teach or demand that which you have not. There is currently within these communities no [67]"familial bonding". What is "FAMILIAL BONDING?"

It is the initial love between family members that is borne out of a common experience and a natural affection and affiliation. This process no longer exists in many minority communities. Most houses in these communities are headed by a single female 20 years old or younger, with 3 or more children who is receiving welfare assistance; and she may or may not have finished high school, so she is primarily unemployable, and the father of her children are even less qualified to support her and his children. The result is they both have been born into a perpetual cycle of poverty and despair. So her mother and father, the children's grandparents, who are not yet 40 years old are themselves victims of the same evil cycle of misery. The children learn how to hustle, curse, pimp, and sell drugs at the age of 5 or 6 because mama needs money for her habit, since she is a user and will be dead before her 35th birthday, and the beat goes on. The Lord Jesus tells His church to 'WAKE UP!

HOW HAS THE CHRISTIAN CHURCHES REACTED TO THIS DRUG DILEMMA?

The majority of Christian churches have closed their eyes to the catastrophic destruction of drugs on the lives and families of America in general. The problem is no longer confined to black, brown, and poor in general; it is now in the suburbs, and gated communities in all places. It is as though the church isolated itself from the very problems that they are called by the Lord Jesus to confront. [68]'Where were you when I was hungry, ... thirsty, ... naked, ... sick, ...and in prison?' The local churches have taken out of the neighborhood, and have invested very little into the neighborhood. The Lord is calling us to 'WAKE UP!' and do the work for which we have been called.

---

[67] David G. Myers, Social Psychology; McGraw-Hill, copyright 2003
[68] Matthew 25:31-46;P.810-811 (NASB)

There will come a day of judgment, and judgment will come to the angels of the household of faith; and on that day, we will all have to give an account of our disobedience, and why we were sleeping on the job. The Christian churches must confront the evil that is present on every hand, evil that has penetrated the very heart and soul of our communities. This is the 'fourth holocaust' that is destroying our youth and the church must "WAKE UP!"

There are churches within our communities that have the name and reputation of being <u>alive and well;</u> but to the contrary, they are <u>dead or near death.</u> Churches that gather Sunday after Sunday and have a great and blessed time in the Lord and leave, and bypass the very people that the Lord Jesus has called us to minister. We fall short of that which the Lord has called us; the suffering, the sick, alcoholic, the needy, the widow, the orphan, and the debilitating effects of the drug culture. We don't want to confront these things because they may disrupt the peace and joy that we experience every Sunday; after all, who wants to deal with the stench of a homeless person, or the breath of an alcoholic, or the repulsive vulgarity of a heroin addict? We have a reputation of being alive and well, because we sing and shout every Sunday, and we tell the world that we have been saved, but only in the confines of our sleeping church building. We make a joyful noise unto the Lord in our sleep, and witness to our unsaved neighbors and friends as we drive by on our way to and from the church; Do we tell them about the saving grace of our Lord and Savior Jesus who is the Christ? We think that since we have a great Pastor, great Deacons, great choir, great ushers, and a beautiful air conditioned sanctuary with closed circuit TV, padded seats, splendidly decorated pulpit, and it's all located on an immense campus, we think that we are alive and well; however, if we are only functioning internally, then we are dead externally. This joy that we have never penetrates the walls of our sanctuaries, and is good for nothing that pertains to the evangelical outreach of the Lord Jesus Christ. The world passes by on the outside, and sees the building, but nothing ever comes out of the building that has any impact on their communities. Perhaps our focus is misguided, maybe we should examine where our affiliations reside, do we belong to the local church, or do we belong to Jesus? Maybe we are serving our church, and not the One who saved us; perhaps we have a misdirected loyalty. If we have a reputation of being alive, and never manifest life outside the four walls of the building, then we are of no effect, no use to the Master. We are dead in our sleep and we must "WAKE UP!"

The conclusion of the matter is that the Lord Jesus has spoken to the angels of the 21st century Christian churches: "He who has the seven Spirits of God and the seven stars, says this:'I know your deeds, that you have a name that you are alive, but you are dead. Wake up, and strengthen the things that remain, which were about to die; for I have not found your deeds completed in the sight of my God. So remember what you have received and heard; and keep it, and repent. Therefore if you do not wake up, I will come....." When the Lord comes will we be awake and busy about His business, or will we be dead asleep, and near death? WAKE UP!!!!!!!!

CHAPTER VI

Christian Denominational Sectarianism

(Do Not Hinder Them!; Forbid Them Not!)

Revelation 3:7-13;P.999-1000 (NASB)
"And to the angel of the church in Philadelphia write:
He who is holy, who is true, who has the key of David,
who opens, and no one will shut, and who shuts and
no one opens, says this: I know your deeds. Behold,
I have put before you an open door which no one can
shut, because you have a little power, and have kept
My word, and have not denied My name. Behold,
I will cause those of the synagogue of Satan, who
say that they are Jews and are not, but lie-I will make
them come and bow down at your feet, and make
them know that I have loved you. Because you have
kept the word of My perseverance, I also will keep you
from the hour of testing, that hour which is about to

come upon the whole world, to test those who dwell on the earth. I am coming quickly; hold fast what you have, so that no one will take your crown. He who overcomes, I will make Him a pillar in the temple of my God, and he will not go from it anymore; and I will write on him the name of My God, and the name of the city of My God, the New Jerusalem, which comes down out of heaven from My God, and My new name. He who has an ear, let him hearwhat the Spirit says to the churches

PROLOGUE:

Many of the Christian churches of this day and time continue to expend an enormous amount of time, energy, and money on defending their doctrinal position as valid biblically, as opposed to other Christian denominations. The church at Philadelphia was an exceptional entity that the Lord chose to bless with a word of encouragement. The Lord expresses His absolute authority in the affairs of the Church at Philadelphia. It illustrates a poignant point that should impact the heart, body, and spirit of every church at all times; and that is, He, the Lord Jesus, has the authority and power to execute His divine will over His churches. He states that since the Church at Philadelphia 'had little power, and had 'kept His word', He would allow them greater opportunities to show forth His Love to the world. Since they have been faithful with little power, obedient in His Word', and have not denied the name above every name, the name of Jesus; the Lord says He will open doors of opportunity to them. Even though the church of satan, the liar's congregation, will oppose and try to discourage you; leave them to Me! Satan's congregation will know that I love you, because you have loved Me; and I will make them subjugate themselves before you. It is evident that an obedient church is also a church that will be protected by the Lord.Those outside satanic influences are subject to the Lord's wrath and judgment. So the church that keeps the Word of Christ, and is obedient to the calling of Christ will be blessed. The point is this; that each Christian Church is accountable only to Christ, and each stands on the merits of their obedience to the Words of the Master! Every Christian Church has more than enough sinners in the world that need the Lord Jesus; so there is no need to engage in these denominational disputes! Do not hinder one another, because the Lord will set things in order when He comes!!!

Christian Denominational Sectarianism!
(Do Not Hinder Them!; Forbid Them Not!)

It is apparent that our Lord and Savior Jesus, who is the Christ, as envisioned by the Apostle John while in exile, he is [69]"caught up in the Spirit on the Lord's day." John is being primed for a Christophany that will manifest the apocalyptic revelation of Him who is the Alpha and Omega, the Almighty God. It is He that has all power and authority to open that which is closed, close that which is open; and He alone has absolute power and authority. The message that the Lord is relaying to John has a cataclysmic impact upon the chords of time, space, and history. It is a message that will envision a time of catastrophic tribulations; and will issue into even greater tribulations. It speaks of the time, the place, and the historical impact that these events would have on humanity. These revelations will reveal the consummation of time, and the intervention of eternity into the affairs of man; and God alone will determine who is worthy to pass through His open door into heaven. Those that are unworthy will find His door shut. Thank God that the opening and closing of the doors to Him are in His hands and not in the hands of man. We have a tendency to open doors to those of whom we are likemind, and close doors to those who are of

---

[69] Revelation 1:10;P.998 (NASB)

a different persuasion. We 'openeth' and 'closeth' doors according to our preconceived concepts of what one Christian denomination believes, as opposed to what another Christian denomination believes. I refer to this phenomena as 'Christian Denominational Sectarianism' because these schisms have become critical in much of Christendom today; but there is no ambiguity in what our Lord says to the church in Chapter 1, verse 8: "I know your deeds. Behold, I have put before you an open door which no one can shut,.." It is amazing that so many local Christian churches attempt to close doors on other Christian churches based on their denominational distinctives. I propose a point of clarification as it concerns this issue, and that is what does the Lord Jesus say:

> Mark 9:38-41;P.825 (NASB)
> "John said to Him, Teacher, we saw someone casting out demons in Your name, and we tried to prevent him because he was not following us. "But Jesus said, "Do not hinder him, for there is no one who will perform a miracle in My name, and be able soon afterward to speak evil of Me. For he who is not against us, is for us. For whosoever gives you a cup of water to drink because of your name as followers of Christ, truly I say to you, he will not lose his reward."

I love the King James, Mark 9:39, wording that says, "him not", don't hinder him. Even with our best intentions, become a stumbling block to those who are observing and li our negative comments about other denominations. Whe among ourselves, we are diametrically opposed to what th has mandated. The lord says that authority is His alone, is the Door, then He will determine who or what, if any, is right or wrong. You do know that we do not have th another man's servant, Paul speaks:

Romans 14:4;P.924 (NASB)
"Who are you to judge the servant of another? To his own master he stands or falls; and he will stand, for the Lord is able to make him stand."

All who have truly professed a saving belief by faith in the salvific sacrifice of Christ Jesus belong to Him, and not to a denomination, not to a Pastor/angel, not to a preacher, but we belong to Christ Jesus alone, and He said "forbid them not!", leave them be. I hope you know that there is no segregation in heaven, a spiritual body will not have skin pigmentation, it won't be necessary, hallelujah, oh praise His name! No one will be admitted because they were Catholic, Baptist, Methodist, Presbyterian, Pentecostal, Episcopal, A.M.E., C.M.E., C.O.G.I.C., or any other denomination. No one made it in because of good looks, no one got in because they were rich, or poor, not because of the color of their skin, not because of who they knew, nor because you are in Who's Who; but everyone got there by the same Door, and that Door is Jesus. He said, [70]"I am the Door: if any man enters through me, he will be saved, and will go in and out, and find pasture." Your denominational distinction will have no bearing on your destination, you must have an intimate relation with the doorkeeper.

There is within many Christian churches an attitude that their denominational distinction, or church doctrine, is true and correct; and all other denominations' tenants, that they deem to be in opposition to their belief, are erroneous. Some even relish with glee the opportunity to verbally attack the doctrinal distinctives of other Christian churches. There is a constant barrage of fierce verbal denunciations concerning those doctrinal issues that they see as different. Most denominations are guilty of quoting selective Scriptures that support their particular distinctiveness; but totally disregard Scripture that opposes their interpretation and

---

[70] John 10:9;P.874 (NASB)

application of the same. Many of the media ministries spend an inordinate amount of time and effort espousing what they perceive as erroneous teachings of other denominations; and some of the radio and television ministries expend an inordinate amount of energy and time berating those of opposing persuasions. Some are so entrenched in church traditions, rather than sound Holy Bible based teaching, that the truth is never considered. Denominational sectarianism was never taught by our Savior the Lord Jesus Christ. The Biblical truths of the Gospels do not support denominational sectarianism; but rather, every person that has accepted the saving grace of the Lord Jesus, as manifested in the vicarious atonement of His sacrificial death on the cross at Calvary, has been baptized into the same body, as one. [71]"There is neither Jew nor Greek, there is neither slave nor free man, there is neither male nor female; for you are all one in Christ Jesus." The Lord has spoken through His Word, "Do not hinder them"; literally He is saying, 'let them be'; 'let them alone'. Stop investing our time and energy on fruitless endeavors that will only render a spiritual deficit. Christ Jesus is speaking to all Christian disciples, in Mark 9:38-41, that you have not the spiritual capacity to comprehend all that He is actively fructifying. The totality of the works of Christ are infinite and eternal, they have no bounds. Catholics and Protestants should discontinue the malicious diatribe that we hurl at one another, as an attempt to validate what we believe to be the truth. There is only one truth, and [72]'If we know the Truth, then we will be free from the prison of sectarianism. Perhaps if we tend to our own denominational distinctives, and preach and teach Christ to our own memberships, then the kingdom of God would be exalted and enriched, but never hindered. It would greatly benefit the kingdom's work, if we teach and preach the commonality of all Christian churches, which is a saving faith in Christ Jesus. We must be cognizant of the fact that the Lord Jesus allows other denominations to exist, and we are called to love and respect one

---

[71] Galatians 3:28;P.948 (NASB)
[72] Reference: John 8:32 (NASB)

another in the Spirit of Christ. We should imitate and emulate the same spirit of love that He gave for us. If we adhere to these, then the Lord Jesus will empower the local church, His church; and enable it to transcend mere denominational sectarianism and manifest His love and saving grace, exceedingly above all that we, as His servants, could ask or even imagine, but, "Do not hinder them!"

The local Christian congregations need to take care of our own local denominational church doctrine and leave other denominational doctrines alone. If your church is doing the soul saving evangelical outreach of Christ Jesus, and considers that the work of the kingdom is an emergency; then there is no time to antagonize each other with what we perceive doctrinal differences. The Lord Jesus has commissioned His churches to become the literal incarnation of Himself. The church should manifest a visible, audible, representation of Jesus, as He did while incarnate in the world. If the church is dedicated to serve Him, then we, [73]"should show forth the praises of Him who has called you out darkness into His marvelous light;..". Our calling is to maximize the spiritual potential of the Christian Church by creating an atmosphere conducive to persuading the lost sinner that Jesus Christ is the way the Truth and the Life. The task of introducing Christ to the unsaved masses requires assets; such as, planning, time, money, and persons dedicated and called to serve God and the lost. If the church is providing clothes for the naked, feeding the hungry, [74]"a cup of cold water" to the thirsty, visiting the sick, and imprisoned, aiding and loving the orphans and widows; then all our time and energy will be exhausted in fulfilling the purpose for which we were called. Surely then we will let other denominations be what the Lord Jesus will allow them to become, "Do not hinder them!"

---

[73] Reference:I Peter 2:9; (NASB)
[74] Reference: Matthew 10:41 (NASB)

INTERLUDE #1

If we do not cease the bickering [75]'The gates of hell will begin to prevail against us'; and the Lord "will come quickly." Satan and his demonic forces have unleashed a full assault against the body of Christ, and we must 'persevere and endure' for His name sake. Satan still attempts to usurp the power and sovereignty of Jesus, but the spiritual war has already been won. Satan will not prevail though he seeks every opportunity to cause divisions and disharmony between the various sects of Christianity. Let us not degrade one another, but surmise that we are confronted by the same enemy. We must flee from negativism and embrace the positive affiliation of our oneness in Christ Jesus. If for no other reason than for the sake of Christ, all Christian churches must agree on one Truth, that all true believers must have accepted Jesus Christ as their Lord and Savior. There is no debate on this, without the acceptance of the gift of God, Jesus Christ, you can not be a Christian. You must accept Him, believe on Him, and He will lead you to a higher calling that will cause you to [76]'love one another, even as He has loved us.' It is the love of God through Christ Jesus that will allow us to rise above denominational sectarianism.

The second point is we need to teach and preach the commonality of all Christian churches, which is a saving faith in Christ Jesus. We are called to be servants of one Master and that is the Lord Jesus Christ; to preach and teach His gospel message, which is Christ crucified, his death, burial, resurrection, and return. It is the good news of what He accomplished for all who would believe in Him; He has secured a means of [77]'reconciliation' to the Father. We are reconciled, brought back into a proper relationship with the Father, by the blood of the Son, Jesus Christ. It is a message that is borne by the power of the indwelling Holy Spirit. The very essence of the Gospel message manifests the love of God borne through the

---

[75] Reference: Matthew 16:18 (NASB)
[76] Reference: John 13:34-35 (NASB)
[77] Reference: Romans 5:11 (NASB)

cataclysmic intervention of Jesus Christ upon the chords of time, space, and history. He removed the crimson stain of sin and death by His shed blood and death on the cross at Calvary, which was sufficient as a propitiation for our sins. This was a gift for all, and not for one or a few, but for everyone who is willing to believe in Him. While denominationally we debate the merits or demerits of baptismal regeneration, the worth of speaking in an unknown tongue, or whether we baptize by sprinkling, submerging, or not at all; and not to mention whether any of the aforementioned are required for salvation. "Do not hinder them!"

That is the message that Christ has for us today. The Apostle Paul observed that within the Church at Corinth there were schisms within the body of believers; [78]some said they were of Paul, and some of Apollos, some of Cephas (Peter) and some of Christ, but has Christ been divided? Paul was not crucified for you, was he? Stop arguing about denominational divisiveness, and ask yourself, what about Jesus? What about Love? Paul said:

> I Corinthians 12:31b & 13:1,2;P.934 (NASB)
> "And I show you a still more excellent way. If I speak with the tongues of men and of angels,but do not have love,I have become a noisy gong or a clanging cymbal. If I have the gift of prophecy, and know all mysteries and all knowledge; and if have all faith, so as to remove mountains, but do not have love, I am nothing."

The love of Christ covers a multitude of sins, and we are all saved by the grace of God, [79]"for by grace you have been saved through faith, and that not of yourselves, it is the Gift of God, not as the result of works, so that no one may boast." If God had given salvation to us according to works, then perhaps some could boast about self efficacy;

---

[78] Reference: I Corinthians 1:12-13 (NASB)
[79] Ephesians 2:8-9;P.950 (NASB)

but there is nothing apart from faith and acceptance of Jesus Christ that we must do. Oh, what a good, good, good God we serve!!! "Do not hinder them!"

INTERLUDE # 2:

The altruistic Love that is manifested by the Gift of God's grace, is the greatest act of compassion to ever intersect into the dimension of time, and that Love is eternally available to be received by whomsoever will! I surmise that the only juxtaposition of God's love, in the realm of human possibilities, is the love of a mother for her infant child. A real mother's love has no bounds or limits to the sacrifices that she would endure for the welfare of her child. No matter the moral state, no matter that they are unworthy of love, and even if they do not reciprocate that love; mama still loves them. Most mothers would give her life for her child. Yes, she would give her life for her own, but for no other. BUT the Bible speaks:

> Romans 5:6-8; P. 918 (NASB)
> "For while we were still helpless, at the right time Christ died for the ungodly. For one will hardly die for a righteous man; though perhaps for the good man someone would dare even to die. But God demonstrates His own love toward us, in that while we were yet sinners, Christ died for us."

There are a multitude of anomalies in this analogy, but what is initially mind boggling is that the mother, perhaps, would die for one or more of her children; but Christ died for every sinner, that is everyone, every soul that has lived, or will ever live. Let me really blow your mind; what religion, what other god, or gods would take on human flesh and die for the sinners of this world, but my God loved us so deeply that He suffered the shame and humiliation of the cross; and the most brutal beating and dehumanizing death. He did it because He loved His step-children enough to die for them. I say we are His step-children because He had only one Son and His name is Jesus. Mama loves us dearly, but God in Christ Jesus loves us more.

Meanwhile, back to the major theme of the previous paragraph, "Do not hinder them", the love of God was bestowed on us through the incarnation of His only begotten Son, Jesus the Christ. God first loved us in spite of our unworthiness, so ought we to love Him and His gift; but we are also called to love one another with the same love that He gave to us. Let us love one another and assuage our denominational differences for the sake of the kingdom of God. There is one tenet that all Christians must accept and believe; and that is, Christ crucified, His death, burial, and Christ risen and He did it because He loves us and seeks to save us. That is the gospel, that is the 'good news' that the Lord God almighty has bestowed on this sinful world because He loves us. "For God so loved the world that He gave His only begotten Son that whosoever believeth on Him shall not perish, but have everlasting life." Christ gave Himself for us all, so "Do not hinder them."

INTERLUDE #3:

All Christians should be cognizant of the fact that Christ Jesus has allowed all Christian denominations to exist in spite of our denominational sectarianism. The 'he who is not for us is against us' attitude is not applicable to the relationship that we who are brothers and sisters in Christ Jesus should exercise. Let me propose some valid reasons why the Lord Jesus allows this situation to persist; first it eliminates the popular excuse that 'I can't find a church that fits who I am.' Because there are so many denominations that lack spiritual maturity, and there are some at different stages of maturity. There are a multitude of churches that will address and fulfill your spiritual needs in Christ. There are preaching churches, teaching churches, singing churches, holier than thou churches, finger popping, hand clapping, boogie woogie churches; no matter what your particular palate of worship might be, there is a church for you. Second, we need to stop sending other denominations to hell, whose doctrines do not agree with ours. Don't be too assured that you won't arrive at the same destination that you are assigning others. [80]"Who are you to judge the servant of another? To his own master he stands or falls; and he will stand, for the Lord is able to make him stand." [81]"But you, why do you judge your brother?' Or you again, why do you judge your brother with contempt? For we will all stand before the judgment seat of God." It is the Lord that will determine who is right and who is wrong, 'He will separate the wheat from the chaff'. So do not hinder them! Third, we need to take care of our own denominations and leave others to Christ Jesus. We, as finite individuals, have not the cognitive, nor spiritual capability to comprehend the totality of the Master's works. Remember in Mark 9:38-41, John, on behalf of the disciples, complained about others that were doing good works, but were not following US. The disciples may have misunderstood the lesson Jesus was teaching; and that following them would never accomplish good works, so if they are doing good, they must be following Me, and I AM aware of all good works!! Jesus was saying that we as mortal beings, have an imperfect knowledge of the aggregate actions of God; and because of this spiritual handicap we should be careful in our judgment of others. Remember that the Lord knows all about all denominations and it is to Him, not us, that they are, and will be accountable. "Do not forbid them."

Finally, when we respect each other denominationally; by, through, and with a spirit of love, Christ Jesus will empower us to transcend mere denominational differences and show forth His grace toward us, and others, exceedingly abundant. In other words, in the words of the noted preacher, who is now with the Lord Jesus, the Reverend A. Lewis Patterson, formerly of Houston, Texas, his new

---

[80] Romans 14:4;P.924 (NASB)
[81] Romans 14:10;P.924 (NASB)

address is heaven; "We need to shut up, swallow our defeats, and broadcast our blessings." We need to 'shut up'; the gospel of shut up should be preached occasionally. If it is a lie, shut up!; if it is hurtful, shut up!; if it is offensive, shut up!; if it is not for the good, shut up!; and if you heard it through the grapevine, shut up! And if it is a stumbling block to others, shut up! After you learn to stop degrading other Christian denominations and shut up, then swallow any bitterness that remains. Swallow and do not regurgitate that which you have put away. Now you can focus those energies that were spent on confrontation and derisiveness of others, and broadcast the goodness of the blessings that the Lord has bestowed on you and yours. Thank God for the victories that he has brought in your life. Simply stated, we need to get rid of a defeatist mentality and broadcast our victorious blessings that can only be found in Christ Jesus our Lord.

> Oh, [82]"what a wonderful change in my life has been wrought, since Jesus came into my heart. I have light in my soul for which long I have sought since Jesus came into my heart"

Broadcast our blessings!, broadcast our blessings!, broadcast our blessings! I am going to tell the world that Jesus is the greatest blessing this world has, is, and will ever receive. He is the greatest Gift from the greatest Giver. Let us cease opposing other Christian denominations and put Christ Jesus at the forefront of our own life and ministry. "Do not hinder them!", "Do not hinder them!", "Do not hinder them!"

---

[82] Song; R. H. McDaniel, "Since Jesus Came Into My Heart"; National Baptist Hymnal, NO.301

CHAPTER VII

Tied-Up Resources: The Lord Has Need Of Them

Revelation 3:14-22; P.1000 (NASB)
"To the angel of the church of Laodiceans write;
The Amen, the faithful and true Witness, the
Beginning of the creation of God, says this:<u>I know
your deeds, that you are neither cold nor hot; I
wish that you were cold or hot. So because you are
lukewarm, and neither hot nor cold, I will spit you
out of My mouth.</u> Because you say, "I am rich and
have become wealthy, and have need of nothing," and
you do not know that you are wretched and miserable
and poor and blind and naked, <u>I advise you to buy
from Me gold refined by fire so that you may become
rich, and white garments so that you may clothe
yourself, and that the shame of your nakedness will
not be revealed; and eye salve to anoint your eyes so</u>

that you may see. Those whom I love, I reprove and discipline; therefore be zealous and repent. Behold I stand at the door and knock; If anyone hears My voice and opens the door, I will come in to him and will dine with him, and he with Me. He who overcomes, I will grant to him to sit down with Me on My throne, as I also overcame and sat down with My Father on His throne. He who has an ear, let him hear what the Spirit says to the churches.

Matthew 21:2,3: P.805 (NASB)
"Go into the village opposite of you, And immediately you will find a donkey tied there and a colt with her; untie them and bring them to Me. If anyone says anything to you, you shall say, "The Lord has need of them and immediately he will send them."

PROLOGUE:

Many of the Christian Churches of today have fallen short of their original intent and purpose; and that is to exist as a living witness to the Gift of Jesus Christ given to a sin sick world. The mission and call of the Christian Church was to minister as Christ Jesus ministered while He dwelt among men, incarnate. Christ was the epitome of Love in human form; because [83]"Greater love has no one than this, that one lay down his life for his friends," and further, [84]"But God demonstrates His own love toward us, in that while we were still sinners, Christ died for us." Jesus died for every true believer in His atoning sacrifice of death on the Cross of Calvary. The Church at Laodicea had become materialistically comfortable, and was spiritually defunct in the mission and evangelical work of the kingdom. They were rich, but

---

[83] John 15:13; P.879 (NASB)
[84] Romans 5:8; P.918 (NASB)

poor; they were bordering on being dispelled by the Lord, because they exhibited none of the traits of His love. They were a church that was idling, they were neither moving ahead, nor reverting; they were more of a social enigma, rather than a spiritual body. They believed that they were self-sufficient and had no need of anything; but what about the Lord Jesus? They had forgotten that it was His church, [85]"I also say to you that you are Peter, and on this rock I will build My church, and the gates of Hades shall not overpower it." There is only one church, and that is His church, and if you are not exhibiting the characteristics that He desires in His church, He may spit you out! Jesus was not an introvert, He went out ministered to the people, and utilized whatever resources the people provided. The saddest commentary that a Christian Church could espouse is that, "we are rich, but we are idle; even though we have tied-up resources that the Lord has need!"

Tied-Up Resources: The Lord Has Need

The Christian churches of the 21st century cannot affo the secular luxury of becoming complacent and lethargic. M churches, like the world, have sought a comfort zone – a st homeostasis. It is the point whereby a church no longer has t or the zeal to be [86]a 'wide door of effective service has opene and there are many adversaries." A church that has become f comfortable because the Lord has allowed them to becom wealthy enough to invest in financial and business prog not relative to the work of the kingdom. These chur invest in business properties, rent properties, stock unions, etc. They have riches, but have not the zes

---

[85] Matthew 16:18; P.801 (NASB)
[86] I Corinthians 16:9; P.937 (NASB)

the kingdom's business. They exist but have no impact upon the lives of anyone outside the walls of their own buildings. They are there, but they are tepid, neither hot nor cold; they are tepid-lukewarm. They are of no real significance within the arena of the Christian calling and mission. They have forgotten who called them, and why He called them. They have taken that which belongs to God and given it to the world. They have refused to be responsible stewards of God's gifts and have tied them up in things that are of no effect, because they are tied-up and cannot be accessed even though 'the Lord has need of them'. The Lord says, "loose them:, and bring them to me". He says, bring it here and 'I will counsel thee to buy of me what you really need, you need gold tried in the fire, you need white raiment;, you need salve for your eyes'. When you receive these you will no longer be tepid, no longer lukewarm; you will become hot for the kingdom's business. You will become 'a vessel fit for the Master's use', because that gift of God that was originally in you will become stirred-up, and the resources of the church will be loosed; no longer will you have tied-up resources that the Lord hath need. The Lord says, 'Come buy from me gold tried in the fire' – gold that has proven itself to be pure, because it has sustained trials and tribulations, endured the flames of temptation and adversity, and has come forth as pure gold. What is gold in this particular instance? It is [87] "so that the proof of your faith, being more precious than gold which is perishable, even though tested by fire, may be found to result in praise and glory and honor at the revelation of Jesus Christ;" Spiritual gold is the byproduct of suffering, and suffering is one of the assurances of salvation. Just as we, who are saved, are to partake of the glory to come with Christ; even so, must we partake of the suffering of Christ. The church that is comfortable because their financial condition is lucrative, is possibly a hell-bound church. The church must purchase the gold of Christ's suffering which cannot be bought with money, but can only be had through showing forth the praises of Him who has brought you out

---

[87] I Peter 1:7; P.986 (NASB)

of darkness. You can be assured that if you show forth His praises, persecution and suffering will come. The reason some of us are so comfortable in our present church affiliation is we; as members of that church, have no impact upon the community where we minister. We are of no effect! The reason we aren't doing anything is we are afraid of upsetting the powers and authorities of this world; we don't want to 'start any mess'. Well, there has always been a mess in the church, there was a mess on the ark, there was a mess in the Tabernacle, there was a mess in the early church, there has always been some mess in the church. Mess is a natural product of spiritual activity. Noah was obedient and granted God's favor, and he had to put up with an Ark filled with animals that were messy.

One of the paramount reasons a great number of local churches are of no import, or impact upon their community is that we have tied-up our resources, money and talent in things that are of no value to the kingdom's business. We want to deal in the currency of this world which will only purchase perishable things. We need to deal in the kingdom's currency, which is the currency used for eternal transactions. And in order to purchase this currency, you need nothing but a willing heart and faith; hence, Isaiah says, [88] "Ho, Everyone who thirsts, come to the waters; and you who have no money come, buy and eat. Come buy wine and milk without money and without cost."Without money, without price – the only resource you will tie-up is yourself, for you must first of all give yourself. When we fully give ourselves to the work of Christ, Christ will empower us to tie-up our resources in Him. The church cannot function properly for Christ if it has tied-up its resources in materialistic investments of no spiritual worth. You cannot buy gold tried in the fire, unless you are actively confronting the wiles of the devil, and the church cannot confront Satan if it has the greater portion of its budget tied-up in bigger buildings, pipe organs, grand pianos, closed circuit TV, intercoms, electronic sound equipment, plush pews, pile carpet,

---

[88] Isaiah 55:1; P.602 (NASB)

modern dining room facilities, etc. Many local churches have taken from their communities, but have invested very little, or nothing into communities. The church of the 21st century, if it is to prevail, must become poor so that the servants of Christ might have life more abundantly through Christ Jesus, our Lord. The church must begin to do the work of Christ in His physical absence. Some churches have tied-up resources that the Lord hath need.

The gold that comes from suffering isn't our only need, we also need the white garments of righteousness. The reason so many of our churches have tied up the resources that the Lord hath need, is that many who are attending are church members, but are not kingdom members. Salvation should first begin at home. A church full of unsaved souls will have the mind of Satan, and Satan is alive and well. He is alive and he flourishes within the church through members who have not purchased the white garments of righteousness. We are all unclothed, naked and utterly shameful when we come before God; wretched, miserable, poor, blind and naked. [89] When we are alienated, cut off from God, we become afraid, but God finds us, much as He did Adam and Eve, and He clothes us. He does not clothe us in animal skins, representative of the Old Testament animal sacrifices of the Judaic faith, but rather God now clothes us in garments of fine white linen, garments that have been washed in the blood of the Lamb. So that when a saint, a true believer in Christ Jesus is looked upon by God, God does not see their miserable, poor, blind, naked, shameful condition; but rather, God sees the garments that His Son has put on those who believe and love Him. The garments of righteousness cannot be purchased at Neiman's, Macy's, Dillard's, Saks, or any high class specialty or common department stores. There isn't enough money in the world to buy these garments, but God will give them to you. The church has tied–up its resources in worldly, perishable investments because many members have not obtained the proper raiment from Christ. There are still some in the church that are

---

[89] Reference:Genesis 3:121 (NASB)

indecently exposed, 'naked as a jaybird'; improperly dressed for the business of the kingdom. So we see nothing wrong with ignoring the <u>aged</u> in our midst, many who are in need; nothing wrong with ignoring the genocidal effects of <u>drugs</u> within our communities; nothing wrong with ignoring the <u>AIDS</u> epidemic, or the drastic increase of <u>orphans</u>, nothing wrong with snubbing the <u>homeless</u> and <u>starving</u>, nothing wrong with prisons predominantly occupied by <u>young minority men</u>, nothing wrong with the inordinate <u>killing of blacks</u> by racist policemen, and nothing wrong with ignoring the <u>sick and infirmed</u>. So we tie-up the resources in materialistic things, and ignore the downtrodden humanity in our communities. The church that ties-up resources that the Lord hath need is probably a hell-bound church that is materially rich and spiritually bankrupt. Tied-up resources that the Lord hath need can lead to a church that suffers from spiritual malnutrition.

Have you considered the place, the building that you refer to as God's house, the place where members can congregate, worship, and praise the Lord? Hypothetically, if God has allowed the church to retire the note on the current facility, and you are having two services each Sunday, and there is still ample seating in the sanctuary; but have you ever considered that God allowed you to retire the note on this building, so that you could untie previously tied-up resources, and invest in community ministries. How does the church that is financially lucrative, that has more than enough, determine that purchasing more material assets is really what the Lord requires? Yes, you are rich, but your wealth has blinded you to the purpose for which you have been called. The Lord said that you leave a bad taste in His mouth; and consequently, He states, "I will spit you out of My mouth!" Yes you are rich but you are of no effect in the 'Kingdom's business'. You have tied-up resources that the Lord needs. There is a possibility that a rich church is about personal comfort and self-aggrandizement? Some Pastors, Bishops, Elders strive to obtain the riches of this world, and all that the world has to offer. They have an elaborate lifestyle evidenced by the best stuff that money can buy; but that evidence will be their conviction when they present themselves at the judgment seat of Christ. 'Those whom He loves, He reproves and disciplines', and He is knocking at the door of your heart; if you let Him in, [90]'He will fellowship with you and reward you, and receive you unto Himself'. Don't allow tied-up resources that the Lord has need, be the stumbling block that prevents you, and the members of your church from being acceptable by the Master.

There is no greater calling for the PASTOR, or ANGEL of a church and its members than they purchase 'garments of fine white linen'; they are symbolic of the righteousness received from Jesus unto salvation. Kingdom currency allows one to purchase gold that has been purified by fire to become spiritually rich. Kingdom currency will allow you to purchase white garments 'to cover your shame and nakedness'; and finally, with Kingdom currency you can purchase salve for your eyes so that you might see. The garments of righteousness are necessary to effectively use the Kingdom Currency that the Lord has provided. We must remember that whatever resources the church has received, they were given willingly to the church. Improper use renders the church of no effect, tepid,[91] 'lukewarm, neither hot nor cold'. The church that has tied up its resources on material things will be spiritually bankrupt; it will have no power to be effective in conducting warfare against the myriad of Satanic influences in our communities.

The 21st century church is composed of both saved and unsaved individuals who come to church most Sundays for a multitude of reasons, and for some, it is not always to praise the Lord. Let us use our sanctified imagination and explore the treacherous journey that every Christian in church has traveled at some time in their lives. Let's say that the 21st century church member is traveling down a major thoroughfare named Satan Avenue, and it intersects with several streets that are major stumbling blocks attempting to prevent them from reaching the intersection of Christ Street and Salvation Boulevard. Since [92]'all have sinned and come short of God's glory'; we

---

[90] Reference: Revelation 3:20-21 (NASB)
[91] Reference: Revelation 3:15-16 (NASB
[92] Reference: Romans 3:23 (NASB)

all start our journey in life on Satan Avenue, also known as Temptations Way. In the journey of life we will cross many intersections; we will eventually cross some streets like Principality Street, Powers Street, Ruler Street, Fornication Avenue, Gay Street, Adultery Place, Idolatry Court, and Liars Corner. Principality and Powers Streets are the primary domain of Satan, and are representative of this world and the evil authorities that reigns over it. It is along this portion of the journey that Satan presents to us [93]"the lust of the flesh, the lust of the eyes, and the pride of life". The spirit of Satan, tries to get us to turn stones into bread (money illegally), he shows the material wealth of this world (fine homes, cars, diamonds, gold, drugs, etc.), and he tells us we can have it all (women, men, prestige, authority, fortune and fame), if we just bow down to him. If we stay the course on Satan Avenue we will come upon Fornication Boulevard, Gay Court, and Adultery Lane; and Satan will be right there to tell you it's all good, and just have a ball. He never tells you that[94] "the wages of sin is death', but the free gift of God is eternal life in Christ Jesus our Lord." The things that he offers have no lasting value, it is counterfeit currency of a bankrupt kingdom, but Christ offers us Kingdom Currency, that will not perish but will lead to eternal life. When the church leaders tie-up resources (Kingdom Currency) on the things of Satan Avenue, Currency that the Lord has need for the work of His Kingdom, then it is lukewarm, tepid, and are no longer effectual for Christ sake. The Lukewarm church needs to remove itself from Satan Avenue and come on over to [95]"Straight Street ', it will show you the way to Christ Street and Salvation Avenue. When you get there you will take off those filthy garments, and put on the white garments of righteousness. Now remember that before you can be clothed, you need to bathe; you've got to be [96] 'washed in the blood of the Lamb.'

---

[93] Reference: I John 2:16 (NASB)
[94] Romans 6:23; P.919 (NASB)
[95] Acts 9:11; P.804 (NASB)
[96] Reference: Revelation 7:14 (NASB)

Now let us not forget the [97]'anointing salve', it is a repellent that prevents the deception caused by 'lust of the eyes'. Once you have purchased and anointed your eyes with the salve that the Lord provides, you will no longer suffer from spiritual myopia. You will see vividly the spirituality of Christ's commitment to His church, as it relates to the church's world wide mission. Christ asks a pertinent question of all saints, [98]"Is there no balm in Gilead, is there no physician there?" Many churches have tied up resources that the Lord has need, and cannot apply the soothing salve needed for the ails of the community. Church members, and the people of the community, come to the local church for assistance with their humanitarian needs; but the church has its resources tied up in material assets and temporal debts. The Lord has provided Kingdom Currency that is sufficient for the mission of the church, but many churches have insufficient funds for the Lord's ministry in communities. Satan has blinded many of the 21st century churches with the stuff of this world. The pastors, the angels of these churches will be held accountable for their lack of obedience to the Lord's command to minister to people. They must not succumb to the philosophy of 'thingalism' or 'stuffism'; nor have a greater desire to be affluent and wealthy by using Kingdom Currency that the Lord has needed. Many have tied up resources to purchase luxurious homes, the finest cars, and go on exorbitant vacations; living high and extravagant on tied up resources that the Lord has need! The Lord will call them to be accountable for their shortcomings. THUS SAITH THE LORD:

Matthew 25:42-43; P.811 (NASB)
"For I was hungry, and you gave Me nothing to eat, I was thirsty, and you gave Me nothing to drink, I was a stranger, and you did not invite Me in; naked, and

---

[97] Reference: Revelation 3:18 (NASB)
[98] Jeremiah 8:22; P.622 (NASB)

you did not clothe Me; sick, and in prison, and you did not visit Me."

If we read the remainder of that chapter, the Lord tells us what their response will be to His indictment:

Then they themselves also will answer, "Lord, when did we see You hungry, or thirsty, or a stranger, or naked, or sick, or in prison, and did not take care of You?"

Then the Lord of life gives an answer to their inquiry:

Then He will answer them, "Truly I say to you, to the extent that you did not do it to one of the least of these, you did not do it to Me."

The Lord Jesus is very explicit about the church's mission to minister to those who are lacking compassion and needed assistance in the communities. So many of the angels, pastors are afflicted by the cataracts of inordinate desire for personal wealth, it has reduced their vision to the point of being blind to the true purpose of their calling. But there is a salve, 'a balm in Gilead' that is available to perform spiritual laser surgery to remove the cataracts of inordinate desire. Once the cataracts are removed they will regain the spiritual ability to seek the righteous will of Him who has called you to manage Kingdom Currency for Kingdom needs.

The conclusion of the matter is that when the pastors and angels begin to untie the resources that the Lord has a need, and use Kingdom Currency for Kingdom needs; then the members and community will be moved to say, [99]"Who is this"? The Word says,

---

[99] Matthew 21:10-11;P.805 (NASB)

[100]"The disciples went and did just as Jesus had instructed them, brought the donkey and the colt, (previously tied up resources) and laid their coats on them; ...." When He had entered Jerusalem, all the city was stirred, saying, "Who is this?"

When the pastors, the angels untie the resources of the church, and use those previously tied up resources as the Lord instructed them to be used; then it will become a 'who church'; rather than a 'what church.' A 'what church', as an inorganic non-entity; but rather a 'who church' that signifies a living viable entity known as the 'body of Christ', His church. A living viable organism that is exuding the very presence of Jesus in its ministry to people. The whole city will be moved to inquire of that pastor, the angel of that church, 'who is this?' They will answer that these are the pastors, the angels of the churches of Christ who have purchased gold tried in the fire, and have become spiritually rich, they purchased white raiment and are clothed in righteousness; and they have purchased salve and have anointed their eyes, and they now see. They could only do this, when they untied the tied up resources that the Lord has need, and applied them to the Kingdom of God in His name; His name is King of Kings; Lord of Lords; His name is Jesus!

---

[100] Reference: Matthew 21:6-10 (NASB)

CHAPTER VIII

Thank God For the 8th Day

Leviticus 23:36; P.101 (NASB)
"For seven days you shall present an offering by fire to the Lord. On the eighth day you shall have a holy convocation and present an offering by fire to the Lord, it is an assembly, you shall do no laborious work."

Exodus 22:29,30; P. 62 (NASB)
"You shall not delay the offering from your harvest and your vintage. The firstborn of your sons you shall give to Me. You shall do the same with your oxen and with your sheep. It shall be with its mother seven days, on the eighth day you shall give it to Me,"

Luke 2:21; P. 836 (NASB)
"And when eight days had passed, before His circumcision, His name was then called Jesus, the

name given by the angel before He was conceived in the womb."

Revelation 22:16; P. 1012 (NASB)
"I, Jesus, have sent My angel to testify to you these things in the churches. I am the root and the descendant of David, the bright and morning star."

Thank God For the 8ᵗʰ Day!!!

EPILOGUE:

The previous seven chapters were concerned with the messages, indictments, and missions given directly to the seven churches in Chapter 2 and 3 of the Book of Revelations; and how those messages relate to the 21ˢᵗ century Christian Church. Those seven epistles are basically an indictment of the shortcomings of those churches; but there are also kudos and blessings for the good that was being accomplished in the name of Jesus. In juxtaposition to the Christian Churches of the 21ˢᵗ century, there are shocking parallels that are clearly in opposition to the mandates given by the Lord to His church. The previous seven chapters exposed some of those shortcomings. Those seven churches are typical of the current state of many of today's Christian Churches, and the various shortcomings that each had. The current and future churches will continue to manifest the same failures. Those seven churches addressed in the book of Revelations, Chapters 2 and 3, were Located in a region known as, [101] Asia Minor; and the epistles were addressed specifically to the churches of Ephesus, Smyrna, Pergamos, Thyatira, Sardis, Philadelphia, and Laodicia." They had been founded initially by the missionary outreach of the Apostle Paul, and occasionally in tandem with John Mark, and/or

---

[101] Reference: Revelation 1:11; (NASB)

Barnabas. The Lord Jesus addressed those epistles [102]'to the angels' of the seven churches of Asia; and parenthetically; and also the number 7 in Scripture is a number that is indicative of completion. The essence is that all churches, at all times, would be recipients of these epistles; and they were to be used for the edification and instruction by Pastors and angels of all Christian Churches.

Many theologians believe the Pastors and angels addressed were angelic beings assigned as overseers of each church; yet others believe they were the human representatives called and anointed by Christ to be servants and ministers to the saints of all churches. I prefer the latter, that they are the Elders, Pastors, Teachers, and leaders that have authority to serve the Lord's elect. The word 'angel' is singular and not plural, 'angels'. The word angel is also interpreted as [103]'messenger', and those seven letters, or 'epistles,' were addressed by Christ to His earthly messenger(s) at each of the seven churches of Asia. Those seven churches were confronted by the Lord concerning their own transgressions and shortcomings, but they were also encouraged by the Lord for their good works. All of them were in need of deliverance from the sins that had beset them. (1) The Church in Ephesus, though the Lord praised them for their good works; He admonished them for being enticed and drawn away from their first love, but they were guilty of apostasy. (2) The Church in Smyrna was primarily a church that was being persecuted, and were about to be severely tested for their faith. (3) The Church in Pergamos, though faithful, was warned of the dangers of succumbing to the wiles of the world. (4) The Church in Thyatira was given kudos for their love and faithful service; but were warned of the dangers of false teachers in their midst. (5) The Church in Sardis was in danger of dying due to introversion and impotent leadership; (6) The Church in Philadelphia was a church in revival and had not denied the name of Christ, but they were being

---

[102] Reference: Revelation 2:1, 8,13,18 & 3:1,:7 & 14 (NASB)
[103] Unger's Bible Dictionary Gk."*angelos*" meaning-Messenger; p.52; Moody Press, Copyright 1966

assaulted by quasi-jews of the synagogue of Satan. (7) The Church in Laodicea was rich materially, but destitute spiritually; and they were in danger of being dissolved. When we consider the dilemma of those churches, the question comes to mind, is there any good news for 21st century Christian Churches? What is the purpose and reasoning of all the shortcomings in today's Christian Churches? Is there any good news that the saints of the Lord's churches can be exalted into a celebration of great joy, at this moment in time? Didn't the Lord promise; [104]"I will never desert you, nor will I ever forsake you." Through all the persecution, pain, failures, and heartache, and utter sinfulness of the whole earth; every faithful church will have its day of repentance, joy, and happiness! Thank God that each of those seven churches would have its Sabbath Day of rest and deliverance; (Day-1) Sunday is Ephesus Day, (Day-2) Monday is Smyrna Day, (Day-3) Tuesday is Pergamos Day, (Day-4) Wednesday is Thyatira Day, (Day-5) Thursday is Sardis Day, (Day-6) Friday is Philadelphia Day, and (Day-7) Saturday is Laodicea. Ephesus was a loveless church; Smyrna was a persecuted church; Pergamos was a compromising church; Thyatira was a corrupt church; Sardis was a dead church; Philadelphia was a faithful church; and Laodicea was a lukewarm church; but thanks be to God that after granting each of these churches their day; that after the 7th day there is an eighth day. The 8th day in the Bible is a day of worship, thanksgiving, and deliverance. We are bombarded everyday with the bad news from major network news sources; but there is good news from another network. The Lord says, that though you may have fallen short for 7 days, everyday of the week; there is an 8th day coming when the Lord Jesus will come with blessings and deliverance.

Leviticus 23:36; P.101 (NASB)
"For seven days you shall present offerings by fire to the Lord. On the eighth day you shall have a holy

---

[104] Hebrew 13:5b; P. 982 (NASB)

convocation and present an offering by fire to the Lord, it is an assembly. You shall do no laborious work."

In the Old Testament the days of celebrations and gatherings by the Jews, and many of the observances relative to the deliverance of the nation were anticlimactic until they observed a high and holy 8th day of communing with the Lord. [105]The Feast of Tabernacles or the Feast of Booths was reminiscent of what the Jews experienced in the wilderness after their deliverance from Egyptian bondage. The true significance of the 8th day throughout the Old Testament is that it is a foreshadowing of a Christophany that is eternally present. A Christophany is an appearance or intervention of Christ into the realm of time from eternity. A manifestation of Jesus the Christ is indelibly foreshadowed from Genesis to Malachi, and is revealed on the 8th day when the baby Jesus was circumcised:

> Luke 2:21; P. 836 (NASB)
> "<u>And when 8 days had passed,</u> before His circumsision, His name was then called Jesus, the name given by the angel before He was conceived in the womb."

Jesus Christ is the fulfillment of the 8th day, which was imposed after a week long observance and celebration of deliverance by the children of Israel. The Jewish Sabbath was observed on Saturday, which was the 7th day, so the 8th day is actually Sunday; and every Christian knows that the resurrection of the Lord Jesus occurred on a Sunday. On the 8th day Jesus was circumcised in fulfillment of the Abrahamic Covenant and began His earthly ministry. It is in Christ that all who believe in Him can experience a new beginning; and every church, and every believer can experience the 8th day with great joy and praise to the One that has secured our souls salvation.

---

[105] Reference: Leviticus 23:33-43 (NASB)

One day when all of the saints march into His eternal presence; what a marvelous and blessed day that will be! Thank God that on the Sabbath Day the Lord Jesus rested in a borrowed tomb, but on the 8th day He rose from the dead, and is alive forever more!

> [106]"They crucified my Savior and nailed Him to the cross,
> They crucified my Savior and nailed Him to the cross,
> They crucified my Savior and nailed Him to the cross,
> And the Lord shall bear my spirit home.
> He 'rose, He 'rose, He 'rose from the dead,
> He 'rose, He 'rose, He 'rose from the dead,
> He 'rose, He 'rose, He 'rose from the dead,
> And the Lord shall bear my spirit home.

Note: All Scripture unless otherwise note is taken from *New American Standard Bible;* Copyright 1960, 1962, 1963,1968,1971-1973, 1975, 1977, 1995 by The Lockman Foundation, Published by Zondervan; Grand Rapids, Michigan 49526, U.S.A.

---

[106] The New National Baptist Hymnal; Copyright 1977 Triad Publications; Hymn #104, "He Arose".